THE MAMAS & THE PAPAS

Michelle Phillips, John Phillips, Denny Doherty, Cass Elliot.
(Photo by Guy Webster)

THE MAMAS & THE PAPAS

california dreamin'

by Doug Hall

QUARRY
MUSIC
BOOKS

The book *The Mamas & The Papas: California Dreamin'* is in part based on
interviews conducted for the authorized video biography "Straight Shooter:
The Mamas & The Papas," produced by Hallway Productions Inc. The quotation
of lyrics from songs cited in the book is intended to illustrate and support the
information and criticism presented by the author and thus constitutes fair use
under existing copyright conventions. Every effort has been made to notify
the publishers of these songs that the lyrics have been quoted in this context.

Special thanks from the publisher to Jim Brown for editorial assistance, and to
Alicia for her assistance in transcribing lyrics.

The publisher gratefully acknowledges the support of the Government of Canada,
Book Publishing Industry Development Program, Department of Canadian Heritage.

ISBN 1-55082-216-0

Design by Susan Hannah.
Typeset by Robert Stewart.
Cover photographs by Guy Webster.

Printed and bound in Canada by AGMV Marquis,
Cap-Saint-Ignace, Quebec.

Published by Quarry Press Inc.,
PO Box 1061,
Kingston, Ontario,
K7L 4Y5 Canada.

www.quarrypress.com.

CONTENTS

The Mamas and The Papas live at the Waldorf Astoria during their induction into the Rock and Roll Hall of Fame. (Photo by Kevin Mazur)

THE MAMAS & THE PAPAS

PREFACE

W hen The Mamas and The Papas took the stage at the Waldorf Astoria Hotel on 12 January 1998 to celebrate their induction into the Rock and Roll Hall of Fame by performing their signature song, *California Dreamin'*, a performance broadcast on VH1 a week later, there were few of us who did not fondly recall the 1960s music scene or wish wistfully that we had been there. Counterculture, Flower Power, Monterey Pop, The Summer of Love — these words were invested with great cultural significance at the time and have taken on even more in the intervening three decades. The 'Age of Aquarius' seems to dawn again each time we hear those unforgettable first lines from *California Dreamin'*:

All the leaves are brown
And the sky is gray
I've been for a walk
On a winter's day
I'd be safe and warm
If I was in L.A.
California dreamin'
On such a winters's day . . .

As the distinctive guitar intro gives way to these hauntingly familiar lyrics, the baroque filigree of John Phillips' famed vocal arrangement evokes images of San Francisco nights and Haight Ashbury days. Images forged right here on the streets of New York City where Phillips was inspired, one cold winter afternoon in 1963, to write the song that came to symbolize the California way of life.

When *California Dreamin'* is played with hits like *Monday, Monday, I Saw Her Again, Words Of Love, Go Where You Wanna Go,* and *Creeque Alley,* there is little question that The Mamas and The Papas significantly shaped the sound of their era, the first American band in the 1960s to rival The Beatles for popularity, not only in the United States but also in the United Kingdom. Like The Beatles, they, too, influenced the look of young America, the first highly popular band to appear in classic hippie attire. A recent press release announcing the appearance of the band in England begins, "Sixties hippie chicks with a pair of white plastic thigh highs and a floral mini at the back of the wardrobe will be able to give them a well-deserved airing because The Mamas and The Papas are back!" Indeed, in the wake of their Hall of Fame induction, MCA Records released a new CD, THE MAMAS AND THE PAPAS: GREATEST HITS, featuring a new interview with Michelle Phillips, a fine complement to their two CD boxed set, CREEQUE ALLEY: THE HISTORY OF THE MAMAS AND THE PAPAS, released in 1991. The popularity of their music has never been higher since The Mamas and The Papas disbanded in 1968.

During the same ceremony, Fleetwood Mac were also inducted into the Hall of Fame. If The Mamas and The Papas were instrumental in defining the sound of the late 1960s in America, Fleetwood Mac, likewise, shaped the sound of the 1970s, a musical relationship recognized by Mick Fleetwood. "The Mamas and The Papas were very much a harmony band," Fleetwood comments. "They had the ability of not just having this one specific sound. They used the girls or Mama Cass or John's voice. That's something that we were able to do with Fleetwood Mac. A lot of The Mamas and The Papas' records were able to really go out in different directions vocally — to never get boring. I think it's a real refreshing thing to have. It's a useful tool, I know that. The Mamas and The Papas were the first male/female vocal ensemble that really hit big. We had not been exploring, to any great extent, vocal harmonies up until then, so it was a definite change in Fleetwood Mac and for sure we were compared stylistically, in terms of what happened. I don't think it went a whole lot further than that point and it certainly doesn't bother me when people say that Fleetwood Mac were The Mamas and The Papas of the '70s. I think there is a comparison."

The male/female vocal ensemble Fleetwood refers to was the arrangment of four voices by John Phillips — the voices of Denny Doherty, Cass Elliot, Michelle Phillips, and John himself. Denny Doherty was born in Halifax, Nova Scotia in 1941 and started playing in a band called The Hipsters in 1957. He became a member of The Colonials before moving to New York and changing the name of the band to The Halifax Three. He became part of the Greenwich Village hootenanny and folk music scene, eventually teaming up with fellow Canadian Zal Yanovsky, Jim Hendricks, John Sebastian, and Cass Elliot to form The Mugwumps. Zanovsky and Sebastian would go on to form the Lovin' Spoonful, Doherty and Elliot would become "Papa" Denny and "Mama" Cass.

Cass Elliot was born Naomi Ellen Cohen in 1941 and grew up in the Washington, DC environs, where she performed in musicals before moving to New York. In 1962, she competed with Barbra Streisand for a part in *I Can Get It For You Wholesale*. Along with Tim Rose and Jim Hendricks, she formed The Triumvirate, a folk group, later renamed The Big Three, and made numerous television appearances with network shows. Two albums were recorded before the group added Denny Doherty and called themselves Cass Eliott and The Big Three. Zal Yanovsky took Tim Rose's part when Rose left the group and their name became The Mugwumps.

John Phillips first met Denny Doherty while he was touring with The Halifax Three and John was performing with The Journeymen. Phillips was totally blown away by Denny's voice: "He had this velvet, liquid voice, someone like Bing Crosby, so good — it still is. Denny is one of the greatest singers in the entire world." Before forming The Journeymen, Phillips had enjoyed considerable success with his folk trio The Abstracts, who changed their name to The Smoothies.

While performing with The Journeymen in San Francisco, John met Michelle Holly Gilliam. Born in Long Beach, California in 1944, Michelle lived a nomadic life with her father after her mother died, moving from from California to New York to Mexico and back to

California. She was still in her mid-teens when she caught the eye of John in San Francisco's Hungry i. John and Michelle were married, and John invited her to perform with him and Denny Doherty as The New Journeymen. Denny, in turn, introduced Cass to John and Michelle.

Along with a quick wit, Cass brought a true, clear, soaring soprano voice to the group. Michelle was three years younger than Cass and less accomplished as a singer, though her radiant beauty made her one of the most attractive singers performing in the 1960s. Michelle readily admits that vocally she was in Cass's shadow with her light soprano, but she learned from Cass, eventually developing a voice with the power and projection to carry the solo parts in songs like *Dedicated To The One I Love.* "She made me sing better than I would ever have sung," Michelle observes. "That would apply to anyone Cass sang with. She was that good — I was lucky to have been there." Denny's blithe spirit, off-the-wall humor, and storytelling skills added to this mix of personalities. As Michelle once observed, "he had a whale of a time being a Papa." These Mamas and Papas were also crossed lovers: John loved Michelle, Cass loved Denny, Denny and Michelle were lovers, and so on. Their intra-band and extra-group relationships strike us now as the epitomy of "free" love.

These were the voices and the personalities John Phillips arranged around his music. While he may have preferred staying in the background, with his first musical love being arranging, John wrote the majority of the songs The Mamas and The Papas recorded and assumed the mantle of lead Papa in the recording studio, on stage, and during contract negotiations. In the recording studio, veteran session players and orchestra conductors marveled at his ear for music; unlike many arrangers who concentrate on one musical genre, John is as adept in arranging folk, jazz, ballads, and cabaret as he is in arranging chart busting pop hits. The eldest member of the band, John always thought of himself as a kind of "Papa," someone you could depend on. The course of his life, especially following the break-up of the band, proved otherwise, however.

John Phillips also played a central role in shaping the culture of his era when he wrote the pop hymn *San Francisco (Be Sure To Wear Flowers In Your Hair),* which Scott McKenzie took to Number 1 in 1967, and when he worked with record producer Lou Adler and Michelle Phillips to organize the first full-scale music festival in America, The Monterey International Pop Festival, which brought such newcomers to the public's attention as Janis Joplin and Jimi Hendrix. Like Joplin and Hendrix, he lived the infamous sex, drugs, and rock'n'roll lifestyle to the maximum, though unlike many of his contemporaries, he stayed alive and still performs today with a version of The Mamas and The Papas. The story of The Mamas and The Papas is thus very much the story of John Phillips. And this story is in many ways the story of an era in 20th-century pop culture.

During the early weeks of 1966, *California Dreamin'* was more than just another single charted high on Top 40 AM radio. The song was a banner announcement trumpeting the news that the times were a-changin', something that the poet laureate of the folk movement, Bob Dylan, had predicted. Along with the equally dreamy visions conjured up by *Monday, Monday* and the promise offered in the folk-pop opulence of recordings like *Dedicated To The One I Love, California Dreamin'* worked better than a string of billboards erected along interstate highways from New York to L.A. could have ever done to advertise the fact that something unique was happening on the West Coast.

Along with their friends The Lovin' Spoonful and fast-breaking folk rock groups like Simon & Garfunkel and The Byrds, The Mamas and The Papas presented a fresh sound and attitude for the 1960s, heralding the dawn of the Age of Aquarius, which astrologers say will be with us for the next 2,000 years. And just as the cultural upheaval and re-examination of values that occurred at the beginning of the Piscean Age set patterns in place that lasted throughout two millennia, the pivotal years of the 1960s renaissance are likely to have set some of the patterns that will shape generations on down the line from where we sit today. One of the most appealing aspects of The Mamas and The Papas was the gender democracy within the foursome, even though they were given their name with reference to the Hell's Angels motorcycle 'mamas'. This was not a band fronted by a single star as had been the pattern set in American rock'n'roll previously by acts like Buddy Holly and The Crickets, Gene Vincent and The Bluecaps, Jay and The Americans, and Paul Revere and The Raiders. In fact, group founder and leader John Phillips retired on stage behind the personalities and talents of Cass, Denny, and Michelle, much as Mick Fleetwood and John McVie would a few years later in their band Fleetwood Mac with Christine McVie, Stevie Nicks, and Lindsey Buckingham fronting. The male/female/male/female configuration of The Mamas and The Papas was in synch with changing attitudes toward women in the music business.

The Mamas and The Papas also had a charismatic group identity like most of the successful British Invasion bands, the kind of charm that put the Beatles over the top into worldwide Beatlemania. Like the Beatles, The Mamas and The Papas set fashion trends, popularizing the hippie wardrobe of the West Coast subculture so effectively that the Fab Four themselves would soon abandon their trademark 'Made-in-London' band jackets, turtlenecks, and high-heeled boots in favor of paisley frocks, bell bottom jeans, and the Nehru jackets popularized by Denny Doherty.

Although based in L.A., The Mamas and The Papas had a recognizable influence on Bay area bands that were forming around this same time, bands like Jefferson Airplane, The Grateful Dead, and Quicksilver Messenger Service, as well as Jimi Hendrix, who would soon graduate from the R&B guitar-acrobatics of his Seattle-based predecessor, Guitar Shorty, and Janis Joplin, who would become the first woman to rock loudly, perfecting the art of screaming musically, belting out her joy and pain on stage while dressed like a street-waif version of Mama Cass. Through their central role in organizing the Monterey International Pop Festival, The Mamas and The Papas were partly responsible for introducing many of these West Coast acts to the nation. Their influence would be felt as far north as Vancouver, British Columbia where groups like The Collectors, Mother Tucker's Yellow Duck, and the Tom Northcott Trio would catch the hippie fever and adopt the Southern Cal fashions. Northcott would come south to record in San Francisco for Warner Bros, where, with producers Lenny Waronker and Leon Russell, he created his marvelous folk-pop version of Donovan's *Sunny Goodge Street*, a record that owes its inspiration to The Mamas and The Papas. *Sunny Goodge Street*, with its circus atmosphere of a lilting calliope collaged into the folk-rock mix, became one of the very first counterculture hits, like the Airplane's *Tobacco Road* or the Dead's *Truckin'* and *Ripple*, that were part of the free-spirited days of early FM radio, but never became Top 40 AM radio successes. While The Mamas and The Papas were AM radio stars, they were also considered hip enough to attract airplay on the underground FM stations, adding to their international acceptance, influence, and success.

The Mamas and The Papas were indeed so successful in packaging the essence of West Coast styles and sounds that — when critics sought a handle to slag them — they would write that the group's sound was *too* packaged, *too* contrived. Nevertheless, imitators of their distinctive folk-pop style were to be heard here, there, and everywhere on the radio, and throughout the era, their hits kept on happening. Following the chart success of *California Dreamin'* in 1966, *Monday, Monday*, their first Number 1 hit, went gold, as did the group's debut album, IF YOU CAN BELIEVE YOUR EYES. *I Saw Her Again* was a summertime smash, peaking at Number 5 during August and hinting at things to come on their much-talked-about second LP. Anticipating a growing demand for that album, their label, ABC-Dunhill, wasted no time in pressing the sophomore effort: THE MAMAS AND THE PAPAS was released to the record stores on October 10th. Once again, the LP went gold, and the third track to chart, *Words Of Love*, hit the Number 5 spot on the surveys. The Mamas and The Papas' third album, THE MAMAS AND THE PAPAS DELIVER, was out in late March 1967, just ahead of that now celebrated summer when the youth of America hit the highway en masse to hitchhike their way back and forth across the nation searching for something better promised in Jack Kerouac's beatnik odyssey *On The Road*. The Mamas and The Papas themselves had made that move westward in 1965, migrating from the Greenwich Village coffeehouses where they had met, gigged, and refined their folk music into the innovative folk-pop style that everybody seemed to want to hear when Lou Adler produced their music for ABC-Dunhill Records in L.A.

The Mamas and The Papas' *Dedicated To The One I Love* peaked at Number 2 in May, and throughout the Summer of Love, they were on everybody's radio dial with all of these songs and a new release they called *Creeque Alley*. They were on stereo decks in customized Chevy vans, paisley-painted VW buses, and big old yellow Bluebird schoolbuses, all loaded with migrant seekers who welcomed the hitch-hiking hordes aboard. A spirit of brotherly love did flourish among the population of runaways, guru-seeking meditators, and just plain and simple kids with their hopes and dreams stowed in a backpack and a guitar case, who were on their way to better times, better situations — a commune somewhere in Oregon or Colorado, or merely to dig some sounds in the West Coast light show palaces like the Avalon Ballroom and the Fillmore West in San Francisco or the Retinal Circus in Vancouver. The youth of America seemed to be taking Dr Timothy Leary's advice and tuning in, turning on, and dropping out.

Creeque Alley told the story of The Mamas and The Papas formative days living this lifestyle. The references to the time they had spent in the Virgin Islands living in tents on the beach, rehearsing and refining their sound, before heading to the West Coast, the mention of their mentors and friends, John Sebastian, Roger McGuinn, and Barry McGuire in the lyrics, all hit-makers in their own right — plus that supremely catchy hook, "And no one's gettin' fat except Mama Cass" — made everyone believe that *California Dreamin'* was becoming a re-al-i-ty.

For that brief moment in time, an 18-month span when they peaked on the U.S. charts with six marvelous records, The Mamas and The Papas outshone everyone, with John Phillips quickly showing not only that he had an exceptional talent for writing songs and arranging music but also for making history by planning the first pop music festival. These talents came together when John wrote and produced *San Francisco (Be Sure To Wear Flowers In Your Hair)* as a move to pacify nervous citizens in Monterey, California where John and Michelle and Lou Adler were hoping to stage the first Monterey Pop Festival at the local fairgrounds. Recorded by John's friend, Scott McKenzie, a former fellow Journeyman, this Top Ten ballad quickly became an early anthem — the signature song — for the flower power generation. Wafting out across America during the spring of 1967, the song was designed to let everyone know that the Monterey Pop Festival was planned as a celebration of music, peace, and love. While the record did not exactly represent the hard-core psychedelic scene that was emerging in the Bay area, *San Francisco* came to represent what most Americans knew about the hippie uprising and the counterculture movement. The festival itself did become a bench-mark in pop culture history, a sort of framing event complemented by the Woodstock festival in 1969.

The spirit of Monterey Pop had been anticipated in the first Human Be-In at Easter. These humans wore flowers in their hair — spontaneously. As David Henderson, author of *'Scuse Me While I Kiss The Sky: The Life of Jimi Hendrix*, reported, "Thousands of young heads had been astonished at the Human Be-In to find thousands of others just like them. All across the country the returns came in on the Be-In. It was like a national election. It read: "We are in power, our shit is working, we can do what we want." Reports of this event were not just printed in the mainstream press, but the proceedings were also reported from a subculture point of view in a growing number of underground newspapers like the *Berkeley Barb*, the *Los Angeles Free Press*, the *East Village Other*, and the *Georgia Straight*. Euphoria was sweeping the nation, eddying out from the Bay area, then felt 'round the entire world after the June 2, 1967 release of the Beatles' SERGEANT PEPPER'S LONELY HEARTS CLUB BAND. Lennon & McCartney had responded to the San Francisco scene with a little California dreaming of their own. John & Paul were also on the board of directors for the Monterey festival.

The first news most people heard about the festival came through the distribution of leaflets at the Be-In. As the date for the music event neared, Derek Taylor, the Beatles' publicist, engineered a successful campaign that, along with Scott McKenzie's record, convinced the mainstream media and the public alike that there was something special going on. The *San Francisco Chronicle* set the stage for the event with this announcement: "The music capital of the world, starting Friday, will be the Monterey Fairgrounds, not Nashville, not Tin Pan Alley and neither London nor Hollywood. The first annual Monterey International Pop Festival is bringing to the Fairgrounds the greatest aggregation of popular song stars ever assembled in any one place for a weekend event." John Phillips and his fellow organizers had done their job. Negativity just wasn't part of the event at all. As Janis Joplin's sister, Laura Joplin, recalls, "the event was organized by John Phillips, one of The Mamas and The Papas, and Lou Adler, a Los Angeles record producer. They envisioned a nonprofit gathering where any money made would be distributed 'for the betterment of pop music' by a board composed of musicians, including Paul McCartney, Paul Simon, and Smokey Robinson. For two and a half days and more than 25 hours of music, the arena was full of peace and love. More than 40,000 people attended, yet Saturday and Sunday, Frank Marinello, police chief, sent 40 uniformed policemen home. They weren't needed. Much more than music was presented; it was high drama. Psychedelic movies played near a midway of booths selling food and paraphernalia. The Who smashed a guitar and Jimi Hendrix — appearing in a gold shirt and red pants, with fuschia feathers around his neck — climaxed his appearance by burning his guitar." The festival was also filmed as a feature movie, the first of its kind.

It was widely reported in the press that Big Brother & The Holding Company were so good that they were called back for an encore set. The reason for that set, however, was more pragmatic. The band's manager, Julius Karpen, had refused to sign a disclaimer permitting the filmmakers to shoot the Saturday afternoon performance of *Down On Me, Road Block,* and *Ball & Chain.* When the band came off the stage and learned of Karpen's action, they were incensed. It was the only ruffle in an otherwise idyllic weekend. As the feathers flew, it became obvious to the organizers that without Joplin's performance on film, they would be vulnerable to critics who could slag the film as having missed the best set. Even Bob Dylan's manager, Albert Grossman, got into the act, exhorting the band to convince their manager to let the film crew shoot their performance. Karpen wanted a cut of the profit, even though all of the other acts were of a single mind to see that money go into a musicians' fund.

As history has recorded, Joplin did go back on, and, along with Hendrix and The Who, stole the show both in the arena and on film. Mama Cass was rendered speechless by Joplin's performance — and that, too, was captured on film. Hendrix was introduced to the 20,000-strong audience by Rolling Stone, Brian Jones, who flew in from London for the occasion. Jones ladled it on and created a huge expectation: "Direct from England! Appearing in the United States for the first time . . . Jimi Hendrix. The Jimi Hendrix Experience!" It was showmanship, a favor Jones performed for his buddy, Chas Chandler, the ex-Animals keyboard player who had put Hendrix together with drummer Mitch Mitchell and bass player Noel Redding to create the Jimi Hendrix Experience.

When Monterey Pop was in high gear, the hard-core groups stole the show. Janis and Jimi and more of their kind showed the world that the San Francisco scene was made of a whole lot more than merely the carefully arranged folk-pop of The Mamas and The Papas. This music was about pulling out all the stops and taking things to never before discovered highs and lows. Soon dubbed psychedelic music, songs like Joplin's *Piece Of My Heart*, the Door's *Light My Fire*, Jimi Hendrix's *Are You Experienced*, and the Airplane's *White Rabbit* would become the new anthems of the generation.

For The Mamas and The Papas, Monterey Pop was a mixed experience. Not anticipating the significance of the event, Denny Doherty very nearly missed their set. Their performance was anti-climatic, feeling more like the end of an era in their careers rather than the apex. Perhaps if the group had been closer in the days and hours leading up to their set, they might have been the ones who were drawing the rave reviews. The cost of John Phillips' concentration on organizing Monterey Pop may have been the beginning of the decline of their fortunes. The Mamas and The Papas seemed to lose some of their momentum. The times kept on a-changin'. FM radio had come to the fore in determining the success of a recording act. Blue Cheer first trumpeted heavy metal. The Doors would set the counterculture ablaze with *Light My Fire*, a longer than usual cut that was shortened for the AM but played full-length on the FM, and set the stage for some *Strange Days* that folks were certainly ready to explore. Jim Morrison was no exponent of baroque ornamentation; he didn't futz around with elaborations at all. He just sang it raw: *Hello, I Love You (won't you jump in my game!)*. The Jimi Hendrix Experience would be the first of several power-trios to psychedelicize their sound: The Cream, three Brits gone AWOL from their Invasion bands, would take the music to new crossroads and beyond. Steppenwolf would soon take everyone on a *Magic Carpet Ride*. By the time that Credence Clearwater Revival hit onto the charts with *Suzie Q.* and *Proud Mary*, the '60s Renaissance had become a full-fledged cultural revolution, which matched the political upheaval of the day. The people who began the fight for Civil Rights and Equal Rights, protested the American presence in the

Vietnam War, and were inspired by Dylan's *Blowin' In The Wind* to march with Martin Luther King Jr. for Peace, for Equality, and all of those other fancy words that were already inked into the U.S. constitution but had been cast aside by generations of rights' abusers . . . those people who had been leaders of the pack were very nearly at the end of a decade of revolutionary duty.

Dennis Hopper, Peter Fonda's partner in the ground-breaking film *Easy Rider* and very briefly the husband of Michelle Phillips after her divorce from John, would later say of these stalwart revolutionaries, "All these guys who became heroes during the sixties lost their position in life. They didn't finish their universities. They successfully stopped a war and started a free speech movement and fought for civil rights, but later became only curiosities at dinner parties. They had no income at all and couldn't really take menial jobs, or felt like they couldn't. What were they going to do? Be busboys? Abby Hoffman became a drug dealer, got busted, went to prison. What a rough way to go. All these guys had leadership abilities, obviously, or they wouldn't have been the leaders that they were during that time. So there's a tragic side to this." To some degree, the same could be said of John Phillips. He may have become so involved in the cultural revolution that he let his band fall apart. The Mamas and The Papas disbanded the next summer; John and Michelle were divorced before the decade ended.

After the group disbanded, John Phillips continued to create music, but he seemed to be a fish out of water in the 1970s, a journeyman without a journey, composing scores for failed films and musicals, writing songs that were never recorded, disappointing his fans, friends, and himself. John's energy dissipated with his enthusiasm for musical exploration, seemingly rendering him vulnerable to hard drug abuse during the 1970s when an ever-increasing supply of highly addictive substances like heroin and cocaine began to consume people's lives.

Like most of those famous superstars who John Phillips helped catapult into the international spotlight, he had been a druggie of the first order in the late 1960s. Sex, drugs, and rock'n'roll *were* the order of the day, pretty much mandatory behavior in those days, whether you were hardcore or pop. Although drug-taking has since either been sensationalized or decried by historians who cast backward glances at the era, you simply had to have been there and done that to know why people like Phillips, Joplin, and Hendrix did what they did. To come to an understanding of what experimentation with drugs held for people living in that decade, it is useful to realize that, for some, smoking pot and taking psychedelics was merely fashionable. For others, it was merely recreational. Still others saw drug use as a a protest against straight society, believing that the laws outlawing these substances would come tumbling down with the impending social and cultural revolution. Few felt any vulnerability to the danger drugs might pose; they were riding a wave of change and often felt invincible. But for many inquisitive and creative people, this experimentation was, at least occasionally, part of a sincere spiritual quest.

Meditation became popular during this period of time and helped foster a popular belief that we are actually on a spiritual quest during our lifetime on the earth. For those who had read Aldous Huxley's *Doors of Perception: Heaven & Hell*, or had discovered Carl Jung's introduction to the Carl Wilhelm translation of the ancient book of intuitive Chinese philosophy, *The I-Ching* or Book of Changes, or who were actively following the lead of spiritual leaders and so-called acid gurus like Dr Timothy Leary or Dr Richard Alpert, there was a belief that an individual could reach a new, higher level of consciousness. There was hope shared among psychiatrists that various psychological ills could be effectively treated with drugs, FDA approved or not. At the same time, some government organizations had come to believe that drugs could be used in behavior modification of a different sort. For more than a decade, since former Nazi doctors and intelligence experts had been brought to North America during the early 1950s along with other experts like rocket scientist Willy von Braun, these agencies had kept their experimentations with brainwashing techniques (designed to be used on spies) and a more ambitious program (that allegedly involved programming assassins) completely out of the realm of public knowledge. By the time some of these experiments were exposed during court cases in the 1980s when former patients sued institutions and doctors for the unauthorized damage done to their nervous systems, the public was tired of hearing about conspiracy theories.

In his book *Flashbacks*, Tomothy Leary recalls that while he was experimenting with magic mushrooms, LSD, and other psycho-active substances at the Harvard University Center for Psychological Research, he spoke with Mary Pinchot, a woman whom Leary suggests was sent to him by John F. Kennedy, and who allegedly took acid with Kennedy. When Leary expressed his belief that not only could you experience God directly by taking acid, but you did so in a highly erotic state that not only created a religious experience but also expanded your intelligence, Pinchot had these words of advice to offer: "The guys who run things — I mean the guys who *really* run things in Washington — are very interested in psychology, and drugs in particular. These people play hardball, Timothy. They want to use drugs for warfare, for espionage, for brainwashing, for control."

During the nearly fifteen years that federal agents had Leary in custody, after arresting him for possession of a small amount of marijuana, they wanted him to, at the very least, identify foreign sources as being responsible for the sixties revolution in America, to which Leary responded, "Your guys in the Federal Bureau of Inves-tigation are making the same mistake that J. Edgar Hoover made and Johnson and Nixon made; trying to blame domestic unrest on foreign agitation. That's all right when you're trying to get appropriations. But it's disastrous to believe your own lie. The counter-culture in this country — the peace movement, the cultural revolution — is not inspired from abroad. It's red-white-and-blue American. The Weathermen, in spite of their Maoist rhetoric, are as American as the Dallas Cowboys."

The "drug wars" that followed the 1960s began as a political slogan created to counteract the negative position the federal government had been put into by the legions of people who had protested American involvement in the Vietnam War and the political climate that brought about President Richard Nixon's resignation during the Watergate investigations. These "drug war" slogans have, however, obscured *all* experimentation with mind-altering drugs by lumping all illegal drugs into one bag. A drug-free America became the goal of most politicians during the final two decades of the 20th century because all drugs have been labeled evil, not because all of them have been proven to be so. Of course, most people have come to agree that substance abuse, whether it be tobacco, cigarettes, alcohol, prescription drugs, or illicit drugs, is not good for anyone.

Strangely, these drug wars coincided with an abundance of water-soluable derivatives of the opium and the coca plants. For people like Tim Leary, these 'hard' drugs held little interest, but for some survivors of the '60s, including musicians like Eric Clapton, George Harrison, Keith Richards, and John Phillips, the mounds of white powders proved to be a temptation that could not be resisted. And in a strange twist of fate, thanks to breakthroughs in treatment techniques started during the 1960s and implemented during the following decades at facilities that specialize in rehabilitation, all of these talented people have come through their own drug wars.

Drugs are not necessarily good *or* bad, they are just drugs. Sometimes it's just a matter of the right drug in the right place at the right time and a person is healed. Sometimes, it is the wrong drug in the wrong place at the wrong time that results in a purgatory worse than a person could possibly imagine, as Dennis Hopper learned through bitter experience: "We can talk about the doors of perception. We can talk about drugs opening doors for us and letting us see on another level, but that door suddenly will close on you and it becomes a black abyss. You're dealing with something that was given to you free to open your doors of perception and suddenly there's a dealer standing at the other end of the tunnel who's selling it to you. Your personal life becomes a nightmare and then you lose both. There's only one way back, to deal with the problem that you have, which most people won't deal with because the drugs and the alcohol are such a euphoric situation that you're in denial most of the time that you have a problem. It's the other people that have the problem. You don't. You can handle it. Anyway, that's my story." In a scary sense this, too, is John Phillips' story during the 1970s when he became a needle-freak, a junkie, and a self-abuser of the worst kind long after John Lennon's celebrated declaration that "the war is over" and long after many of his fellow rock stars had kicked their drug habits. When that "black abyss" finally opened, he was in the midst of recording a comeback album that could have put him back at the top of the charts, working with Mick Jagger and Keith Richards. The failure of that promising project wasn't enough to straighten him out, nor did the drug addiction of his children, actress MacKenzie Phillips and Jeffrey, inspire change. Not until he faced a conviction on charges for interstate trafficking and a sentence of years in prison did John finally pull himself out of his nose dive. His lawyer and his therapist appealed to him to set an example for the other members of his family who had also become substance-abusers; he was, it was suggested to him, more than a little responsible for those people, all of whom loved him and depended on him. Phillips had been on a death trip but couldn't seem to die, the kind of death trip portrayed in *Easy Rider*, with a karmic debt owing from dealing hard drugs, the debt described in Hoyt Axton's song *The Pusher*, recorded by Steppenwolf. "God damn the pusher man."

While commenting on his own drug abuse, Dennis Hopper offers another perspective on John Phillips' case: "Janis died. Jimi died. These people were full of life. These were not people who were on a suicide bent. They thought they could do it and live. They thought other people OD'd. We all did." Yet John Phillips had a special resilience that served him through all of those Purple Haze days, Orange Sunshine sunsets, and Southern Comfort Monday mornings coming down, a resilience shock-jock journalist Howard Stern tastelessly pillories: "Papa John. You compare him with Jim Morrison, John Belushi, and Janis Joplin. *They* didn't know how to take drugs — they died. Belushi. What — he was on drugs for how long, would you say? He died. Papa John was on drugs for how long would you say? Fifteen years? Wrote music. If he didn't get caught, he'd still be going strong. The guy's got incredible stamina. Elvis Presley, of course, was a big embarrassment. The man didn't know how to take drugs. Give him a couple of legal drugs and right away he's making it in his pants, having to wear diapers. Papa John is an inspiration to us all. Now, I don't do drugs, I don't recommend drug use. I smoke a little joint, I get paranoid. I can't even function. Papa John, you give him a joint, give him some heroin, give him some coke, give him a speedball, give him some crack — this guy just keeps going. If the cops hadn't caught him, God knows what Papa John could have taken in terms of drugs — and lived."

An odd claim to cultural fame, perhaps, but buried beneath Howard Stern's hyperbole is a sad irony and an idle thought. If John Phillips had not become a drug abuser, how many more great songs would he have written, arranged, and recorded for The Mamas and The

Papas by now? Perhaps a whole slew. Perhaps none at all. Because, if John Phillips had not been fully immersed in the spirit of the times, he could not have sincerely embodied this era in American pop culture.

By 1969, Crosby, Stills, Nash & Young had taken electrified folk to a different level in recording Joni Mitchell's *Woodstock*, topping some of the 1967 Monterey Pop Festival alumni, like Eric Burdon and his *(Down In) Monterey* release, and they were rivaling Jimi Hendrix, whose rendition of Dylan's *All Along The Watchtower*, along with denser confrontations like *Foxy Lady* and *Purple Haze*, had blown most of the previous preconceptions about what could be done in a recording studio right out the window. Both the Woodstock festival and Mitchell's song marked the end on one era and the beginning of another where Crosby, Stills, Nash & Young, The Eagles, Fleetwood Mac, Led Zeppelin, Joe Cocker, Santana, Sly and The Family Stone, The Plastic Ono Band, and then the whole punk and disco reaction took the stage. A New Age. The 1970s. By the time that Woodstock was over, the love generation was also ancient history. But for a while in the late 1960s, The Mamas and The Papas were the best sound around among American folk pop bands. It was a wondrous sound, resonant with the spirit of the age. A sound to die for.

In 1971, The Mamas and The Papas fulfilled a contractual obligation to Dunhill by recording PEOPLE LIKE US, but the recording sessions at John Phillips' Bel Air home recording studio were a battlefield of conflicting careers and personal jealousies, and the four singers never had their hearts in it — never actually sang together at the same time.

Cass Elliott was pursuing a solo career she had launched with the release of DREAM A LITTLE DREAM OF ME in 1968 while still officially a member of the band. She became a minor celebrity on the TV talk show circuit, but her solo career failed to recapture the magic she had enjoyed as a member of The Mamas and The Papas, even though she recorded several more albums. Cass died tragically and alone in 1974 from a massive heart attack.

Denny Doherty, likewise, tried a solo career, releasing two albums in the early 1970s. Neither was successful. Exhausted from the pressure and turmoil of the music business, Denny and his wife Jeanette moved back to Canada in 1975 where he performed on his own television show. In the early 1980s, when The New Mamas and The Papas were formed, he returned to the fold along with John Phillips and new members MacKenzie Phillips and Spanky McFarlane. In 1996, Doherty and fellow Mugwump, Zal Yanovsky, were inducted into the Canadian Music Hall of Fame. He has performed as the harbor-master host of a pre-school TV show, *Theodore Tugboat*, and in the CBC-TV series *Pit Pony*. For the Neptune Theatre in Halifax, Nova Scotia, he produced with Canadian playwright Paul Ledoux the stage show "Dream a Little Dream of Me," a two-act musical autobiography that recreates the folk rock era of the 1960s and tells the story of The Mamas and The Papas, with Denny narrating and performing such hits as *Monday, Monday* and *California Dreamin'*.

Following her divorce from John, Michelle Phillips appeared in the feature films *The Last Movie, Dillinger*, and *Valentino*. In 1977, she recorded a solo album, VICTIM OF ROMANCE, for A&M Records. She took her role as a mother seriously. Now in her mid-fifties, she continues to appear in films and on prime time television soap operas like the highly-rated *Knots Landing* and *Beverly Hills 90210*.

John Phillips released a solo album, JOHN PHILLIPS: THE WOLF KING OF L.A., in 1970. He next worked on the film soundtrack for *Myra Breckinridge* and wrote the lyrics and score for the Broadway musical *Space*. During the late 1970s, he worked with members of the Rolling Stones on a new solo album, '*Phillips 77*', which was not released. The sessions were marred by lacklustre efforts by both John and Keith Richards whose mutual heroin use undermined the project and signaled Phillips' descent into an abyss of addiction that wiped out his desire to create and nearly ended his life. Following his conviction for drug trafficking, and during his continuing recovery period in 1981, Phillips formed The New Mamas and The Papas and co-wrote *Kokomo* with Scott McKenzie, which became a 1988 Number 1 hit for the Beach Boys. The New Mamas and Papas continue to record such albums as HALF STONED, MANY MAMAS, MANY PAPAS, and THE MAMAS AND THE PAPAS LIVE, and to perform their "Endless World Tour," though the cast changes, with Scott McKenzie, Barry McGuire, David Baker, and others becoming 'Papas' from time to time, and with MacKenzie Phillips, Spanky McFarlane, Chrissy Faith, Janelle Sadler, and others performing as 'Mamas.' Of course, through all of the changes, John Phillips remains *the* Papa. "Everyone is breathing a sigh of relief," says Michelle, commenting on John's ability to continue performing after his many trials — legal and medical, emotional and spiritual — "because he *is* a great man!"

This book is in part based on the interviews and research conducted for the authorized video biography *Straight Shooter: The Story of The Mamas and The Papas,* a Gemini Award winning television documentary and home video, augmented with factual information recorded in the autobiographies of John Phillips (*Papa John: An Autobiography*) and Michelle Phillips (*California Dreamin': The True Story of The Mamas and The Papas*), and in Jon Johnson's biography of Cass Elliot, *Make Your Own Kind of Music.* These books are now out-of-print. Nearly forty interviews were taped on location with the cooperation of the surviving members of the original group, their family and friends, record producers and session musicians, fellow performers and television personalities, their physicians, business associates, and lawyers. Although only twenty-five percent of the information gathered from the interviews could be included in the video documentary, most of the interview content is now transcribed in this book.

The interviews are far ranging. John Phillips' sister Rosie paints a picture of her brother going where he wants to go and doing what he wants to do as a child, while his close friend Bill Cleary tells of their adolescence in a gang called the Del Ray Locals that not only banged heads but also sang on street corners. From *Tonight Show* scriptwriter Marshall Brickman we hear about John's invitation to that fatal party at the home of Roman Polanski and Sharon Tate, where she was murdered along with five other guests by the Charles Manson family. Joe Cocker remembers the extravagant parties held at the Bel Air mansion owned by John and Michelle. Film director D. A. Pennebaker takes us behind the scenes at Monterey Pop, while photographer Guy Webster describes the composition of the unusual cover shot of The Mamas and The Papas posed in a bathtub for their first album. But most strikingly, we hear Denny, Michelle, and John speaking in their own voices, telling their own tales, setting the record straight. This is the cast who present the true story of The Mamas and The Papas, the highs and the lows, the triumphs and the trials — who recreate for us the magic of The Mamas and The Papas and give ample reason for their enduring influence on pop culture.

Accompanying a re-broadcast of the Rock and Roll Hall of Fame induction ceremony for The Mamas and The Papas on VH1, the producers programmed a special "Behind the Scenes" look at the lives and careers of The Mamas and The Papas, to which an old fan responded on the popular "iMusic" world wide web site: "Hey, I saw The Mamas and The Papas special last night on VH1. It brought back a lot of good memories of a truly great California band. Today I've been listening to the GREATEST HITS CD and just enjoying it all. John, Michelle, Denny, Cass, thank you." On the same bulletin board was posted a note from a younger fan: "Hey, I'm 14/m and I love The Mamas and The Papas. I've found all their albums on CD except for THE MAMAS AND THE PAPAS. If anyone has any of their records that they would like to sell, I'm here." The legend of The Mamas and The Papas continues into the next generation.

THE MAMAS
THE PAPAS

CAST

Susan Adams: "Susie" Adams is John's first wife and the mother of Jeffrey and Laura MacKenzie Phillips.

Frank Arraznati: Frank Arraznati produced the album THE NEW MAMAS AND THE PAPAS in the early 1980s.

Hoyt Axton: Hoyt Axton was witness to the San Francisco scene in the early 1960s when he first met John Phillips playing there with The New Journeymen. Axton wrote such diverse songs as *The Pusher*, recorded by Steppenwolf, and *Joy To The World*, recorded by Three Dog Night.

Marshall Brickman: Folk banjo picker Marshall Brickman first played in a little group called The Terriers, then formed The New Journeymen in 1964 with John and Michelle Phillips. He later became a revered comedy writer for Johnny Carson and Dick Cavett.

James Burton: The guitar stylist who created Ricky Nelson's early hits and played on many of Elvis Presley's recordings, James Burton was chosen by John Phillips to work with him on his WOLF KING OF L.A. album.

Dick Cavett: Talk show host Dick Cavett was with John when he heard about Mama Cass Elliot's death.

Dick Clark: Dick Clark, host of *American Bandstand*, recognized when The Mamas and The Papas first played on his show that they were going to have a profound influence on the music scene.

Bill Cleary: Bill Cleary was one of John Phillips' earliest childhood friends, who started singing with John in the Del Ray Locals and ended up facing a drug trafficking charge with him.

Joe Cocker: Recording artist Joe Cocker remembers being at a party at John's house in Bel Air where he was singularly impressed by what he saw.

Pierre Cossette: Record executive Pierre Cossette owned Dunhill Records and signed The Mamas and The Papas.

Denny Doherty: Original Papa Denny Doherty is the source of more good stories about The Mamas and The Papas than anyone else in the group.

Pete Fornatale: Co-author of *Who Can It Be Now? The Lyrics Game that Takes You Back to the '80s*, Pete Fornatale was a college radio deejay when he first heard The Mamas and The Papas.

Dr Mark Gold: Dr Mark Gold, Director of Research at Fair Oaks Hospital, was instrumental in John Phillips' recovery from drug addiction.

Harvey Goldberg: Record producer Harvey Goldberg was only nineteen when he first met John Phillips, who at the time was making some demo tapes with Genevieve Waite, his third wife.

Scott McKenzie (a.k.a. Phil Blondheim): Now a Papa, with The New Mamas and The Papas, Scott McKenzie calls the group "The Travelling Rehab Circus." Scott McKenzie recorded John's song *San Francisco (Be Sure To Wear Flowers In Your Hair)*, the anthem for a generation of Flower Children.

Elaine "Spanky" McFarlane: "Spanky" McFarlane, lead singer for the 1960s group Spanky and Our Gang and one of Cass Elliot's closest friends, became one of the new Mamas when John re-formed the group in the early 1980s.

Michael McLean: Casting director and agent Michael McLean met John Phillips when he was casting the movie *Myra Breckinridge*.

D.A. Pennebaker: D.A. Pennebaker directed the film *Monterey Pop*, which documented The Monterey Folk Festival, created by John Phillips and his colleagues.

John Phillips: Songwriter, musician, arranger, promoter, producer and founder of The Mamas and The Papas, John Phillips is the quintessential 1960s pop artist.

Laura MacKenzie Phillips: The daughter of John and Susan, MacKenzie Phillips became a recording star and television actor (*One Day at a Time*) who became a member of The New Mamas and The Papas.

Michelle Phillips: Holly Michelle Gilliam married John Phillips and became a founding member of The Mamas and The Papas.

Lou Robins: As the manager of The Mamas and The Papas, Lou Robins was instrumental in working out tour schedules and promoting concerts all over the United States and Canada.

Charlie Ryan: New York booking agent Charlie Ryan arranged for The Abstracts (John Phillips, Bill Cleary, Mike Boran, and Phil Blondheim before he changed his name to Scott McKenzie) to audition for Decca Records.

Richard Schaeffer: Criminal attorney Richard Schaeffer defended John Phillips on serious drug charges and saved him from a long prison term.

Jimmie Short: John's boyhood friend Jimmie Short was one of the Del Ray Locals.

John Stewart: Kingston Trio member John Stewart, a close friend of John Phillips, wrote *Daydream Believer*, a hit for the Monkees in 1967, and recorded the solo album BOMB'S AWAY, produced by Lindsey Buckingham of Fleetwood Mac, with Stevie Nicks singing harmony on the Top 5 single release, *Gold*.

Bill Throckmorton: John Phillips' ex-brother-in-law Bill Throckmorton became his first music mentor and whetted his appetite for a career in music.

Rosemary Throckmorton: John Phillip's sister Rosemary ("Rosie") Throckmorton stood beside John when he needed support, though she sided with Michelle in the custody battle for Tamerlane when their marriage ended.

Chris Thurlow: Chris Thurlow and her sister were neighbors of John and Genevieve Phillips while they were living in Connecticut.

Steve Thurlow: Former Washington Redskin football player Steve Thurlow and John Phillips bonded when John and Genevieve moved in next door.

Guy Webster: Guy Webster worked for Lou Adler at Dunhill Records and shot album covers for The Mamas and The Papas.

THE MAMAS & THE PAPAS

CHRONOLOGY

1935: John Edmund Andrew Phillips is born on 30 August at Parris Island, South Carolina.

1941: Dennis "Denny" Doherty is born on 29 November at Halifax, Nova Scotia.

1942: John becomes a cadet at Linton Hall Academy, a military school run by nuns, at Manassas, Virginia.

1943: Cass Elliot is born on 19 September at Baltimore, Maryland.

1944: Holly Michelle Gilliam is born on 6 April at Long Beach, California.

1954: John earns an appointment to the Annapolis Naval Academy, but soon orchestrates his medical discharge.

1956: John receives a basketball scholarship from Hampden-Sydney College but is expelled.

1957: John and Susan ("Susie") Adams are married, and Jeffrey Phillips is born.

1958: John and friend Mike Johnson leave to fight for Castro in Cuba but end up singing in bars and cafes.

1958: John leaves home again and heads for Los Angeles where he sings solo in a number of clubs.

1959: John forms The Abstracts with Bill Cleary, Mike Boran, and Phil Blondheim, who changes his name to Scott McKenzie when Laura MacKenzie Phillips is born.

1960: The Abstracts sign a recording contract with Decca Records, change their name to The Smoothies, appear on Dick Clark's *American Bandstand*, and disband before the end of the year.

1961: John and Scott form The Journeymen with banjo and guitar player Dick Weissman. The band signs with Capitol Records and appears at Gerdes Folk City in The Village on a bill with Bob Dylan.

1961: The Journeymen are booked into San Francisco's Hungry i, where John meets Michelle Gilliam, and together they start writing songs with John Stewart of The Kingston Trio. The Journeymen's first album is released.

1962: Cass Elliot competes with Barbra Streisand for the role of Miss Marmelstein in the Broadway play *I Can Get It For You Wholesale*.

1962: John and Michelle are married in Rockville, Maryland.

1963: The Journeymen's third album, NEW DIRECTIONS IN FOLK MUSIC, is released, they are booked on the Hootenanny Tour with Glen Yarborough, Jo Mapes, and The Halifax Three with Denny Doherty, and play Carnegie Hall.

1963: Cass marries Jim Hendricks to help him escape the draft, and with Tim Rose they form The Triumvirate, a folk group, later known as The Big Three, featuring Hendricks, Zal Yanovsky, and

Denny Doherty before becoming The Mugwumps, with Art Stokes on drums and John Sebastian on harmonica. Sebastian and Yanovsky went on to form the Lovin' Spoonful.

1963: John writes *California Dreamin'* after walking through a snow storm in New York with Michelle.

1964: The Journeymen play The Troubadour in L.A. with Hoyt Axton, John and Scott leave the group, and Michelle and John decide to team up and form The New Journeymen, adding banjo player Marshall Brickman and vocalist Denny Doherty.

1965: Denny introduces Cass Elliot to John and Michelle. John, Michelle, Denny and friends decide to leave New York for The Virgin Islands. John, Michelle, and Denny rehearse as a group and are booked at Duffy's hotel on a narrow street called Creeque Alley.

1965: John and Michelle take a "you drive" car to Los Angeles, and John writes *Straight Shooter* and *Go Where You Wanna Go* en route. They arrive in L.A. during the Watt's riots.

1965: John suspects that Denny and Michelle are involved and writes *I Saw Her Again*, with Denny receiving a co-author credit.

1965: Barry McGuire introduces the group to Lou Adler of Dunhill, who signs them to a contract. The band takes its name of The Mamas and The Papas from the Hell's Angels who call their women "Mamas."

1965: John writes *Twelve Thirty (Young Girls Are Coming To The Canyon)* and *Go Where You Wanna Go* is released as a single.

1966: The Mamas and The Papas have five Top Five Hits — *California Dreamin'* (#4), *Monday, Monday* (#1), *Dedicated To The One I Love* (#2), *I Saw Her Again* (#5), and *Words Of Love* (#5) — and they release two albums, IF YOU CAN BELIEVE YOUR EYES AND EARS and THE MAMAS AND THE PAPAS.

1966: Michelle has an affair with Gene Clark of The Byrds and John "fires" her from The Mamas and The Papas. Lou Adler's girlfriend, Jill Gibson, replaces Michelle, but Michelle reunites with the band to record *Dancing In The Streets*.

1966: John and Michelle's dream home in Bel Air becomes the focal point for memorable Hollywood parties.

1966: The album IF YOU CAN BELIEVE YOUR EYES reaches gold along with their singles *California Dreamin'* and *Monday, Monday*.

1967: The Mamas and The Papas win a Grammy for Best Contemporary (Rock and Roll) Group Performance for *Monday, Monday* and release THE MAMAS AND THE PAPAS DELIVER, their third album. Cass has a baby girl, Owen Vanessa, and *Creeque Alley* moves up the charts to Number 5.

1967: John's song, *San Francisco (Be Sure To Wear Flowers In Your Hair)*, recorded by Scott McKenzie, reaches Number 4 on the US and Number 1 on the UK charts. John and Lou Adler organize the Monterey Pop Festival, where The Mamas and The Papas perform.

1967: Jimi Hendrix opens for The Mamas and The Papas at The Hollywood Bowl.

1967: John announces at a press conference in September that The Mamas and The Papas are breaking up, but at the end of the same week they appear on *The Ed Sullivan Show*.

1968: FAREWELL TO THE FIRST GOLDEN ERA, The Mamas and The Papas' fourth album, is released.

1968: Chynna Gilliam Phillips is born to John and Michelle. Like MacKenzie Phillips she will pursue a career in music with the band Wilson Phillips.

1968: The Mamas and The Papas' single *Safe In My Garden* is released the same week that Robert Kennedy is assassinated.

1968: Mama Cass releases the single *Dream A Little Dream Of Me*, her biggest solo hit.

1968: The Mamas and The Papas disband.

1969: Dunhill Records sues the group over a contractual dispute but then release them from their contract.

1969: John writes music for the movie *Myra Breckinridge* and places his song *Secret Places* on the soundtrack.

1969: John files for divorce from Michelle and meets Genevieve Waite. He records the solo album JOHN, THE WOLF KING OF L.A. and begins working on the musical *Space* (later called *Man on the Moon*) with Genevieve and Denny.

1969: John is invited to a party at Sharon Tate's house but declines. The followers of Charles Manson murder five of the guests, including Sharon Tate.

1970: Cass appears in the film version of *H. R. Pufnstuff* as well as on the *Scooby Doo Cartoon Hour* as the heir of a haunted candy factory.

1970: Michelle appears in the film *The Last Movie* with Dennis Hopper. They marry but break up within eight days. Michelle sings backup for Leonard Cohen.

1970: Cass records *Something To Make You Happy/Next To You* with rock star Dave Mason.

1971: Denny releases a solo album, WATCHA GONNA DO.

1971: The Mamas and The Papas reunite to record the album PEOPLE LIKE US and release the single *Step Out*, which charts in the Top 80 then vanishes.

1971: Michelle begins dating Jack Nicholson. Tamerlane Phillips is born, the daughter of John and Genevieve.

1972: MacKenzie Phillips forms her own rock group and auditions successfully for a role in *American Graffiti*.

1972: John signs with CBC Records and releases the single *Revolution On Vacation*.

1973: Cass releases her solo album DON'T CALL ME MAMA, hosts the *Tonight Show*, and stars on her own show, *Don't Call Me Mama Anymore*.

1973: John accuses his former label ABC/Dunhill of theft from artists who recorded for them (close to half a million dollars is paid back in 1985).

1974: ROMANCE IS ON THE ROOF, John and Genevieve's LP, is released.

1974: On July 29, Cass dies in her London Mayfair apartment following a triumphant appearance at the Palladium.

1974: Denny's second solo album, WAITING FOR A SONG, is released. He is signed as one of the stars of *Space*, which opens in January 1975 but closes within a week.

1975: MacKenzie Phillips appears in the film *Rafferty* which leads to her starring role in the TV sitcom *One Day At A Time*. Her mother begins dating Warren Beatty while acting in *Shampoo*.

1975: Denny moves back to Halifax where he acts on stage at the Neptune Theatre and hosts his own television music variety show.

1975: John and Genevieve become friends with Colin Tennant, Princess Margaret, and her friend Roddy Llewellyn. Nick Roeg, a British film director, invites John to write the score for the film

The Man Who Fell To Earth with David Bowie as the star and he becomes friends with The Rolling Stones.

1976: John and Mick Jagger produce tracks for a projected LP, with Keith Richards, Mick Taylor, and Rebop as guest musicians. Keith Richards, Anita Pallenberg, and son Marlon move in with John, Genevieve, and Tamerlane. John's drug abuse escalates.

1976: Michelle co-stars with Rudolph Nureyev as her lover in the film *Valentino*.

1977: John and MacKenzie get together with Michelle to work on tracks for her first solo album, VICTIM OF ROMANCE.

1977: John begins a triplicate prescription drug scam with K&B Drugs in New York and becomes cross-addicted to heroin and cocaine. High on Quaaludes, MacKenzie is taken into custody by the L.A. Police and receives a one-year suspension from her TV show *One Day At A Time*. John's son Jeffrey and wife Genevieve also begin abusing drugs.

1978: John and Michelle appear with Denny on his television show and briefly consider re-uniting.

1979: John and Michelle battle over the custody of Tamerlane and his sister Rosie is named Tamerlane's legal guardian.

1980: Bijou Phillips is born, the daughter of John and Genevieve.

1980: John is arrested for his part in the K&B Drugs affair. With Genevieve he is admitted to Fair Oaks Hospital in Summit, New Jersey, before pleading guilty to conspiracy and trafficking charges. MacKenzie and Jeffrey enter a drug rehabilitation center. Denny checks into the alcoholic treatment wing at Fair Oaks Hospital.

1981: John and MacKenzie begin making anti-drug appearances on major TV network shows and appear on the front cover of *People* magazine under the headline "How They Kicked their $1-million habit. One Day At A Time."

1981: John's prison sentence of eight years is suspended after serving twenty-four days at the Allenwood Federal Camp in rural Pennsylvania.

1982: John and Genevieve legally separate.

1982: The New Mamas and The Papas, with John, MacKenzie, Denny, and Elaine "Spanky" McFarlane, play the first show of their reunion tour at the Other End Club in New York.

1983: The New Mamas and The Papas disband. John and Scott McKenzie co-write *Kokomo*, which the Beach Boys record in 1988 and take to Number 1 on the charts.

1985: John, MacKenzie, Denny, and Spanky once again revive The Mamas and The Papas and perform in Reno, Nevada.

1988: Hallway Productions releases the authorized video biography *Straight Shooter: The Story of The Mamas and The Papas*, which wins a Gemini Award for Best Documentary.

1990: Chynna Phillips records the Number 1 hit *Hold On* as a member of Wilson Phillips, a vocal and songwriting trio including Carnie and Wendy Wilson, daughters of Brian Wilson from the Beach Boys.

1991: MCA Records release the two CD boxed set CREEQUE ALLEY: THE HISTORY OF THE MAMAS AND THE PAPAS.

1992: Cass Elliot's *Dream A Little Dream Of Me* belatedly hits Number 3 on Germany's pop singles chart.

1992: John recovers from successful hip and liver replacement operations.

1996: Michelle stars in the TV series *Malibu Beach* after a long run on the popular evening soap opera *Knots Landing*.

1996: Denny is inducted into the Hall of Fame by the Canadian Academy of Recording Arts & Sciences, along with his old friend and band-mate Zal Yanovsky. Denny becomes the host of the hit Canadian pre-school TV show *Theodore Tugboat*.

1998: The Mamas and The Papas are inducted into the Rock and Roll Hall of Fame. At the induction ceremony, John, Michelle, and Denny perform *California Dreamin'*.

THE MAMAS
THE PAPAS

GO WHERE YOU WANNA GO

Go Where You Wanna Go

You gotta go where you wanna go
Do what you wanna do
With whoever you wanna do it with . . .

(John Phillips, ASCAP)

Had the American government not undertaken what it termed "The Great Removal" in the mid-19th century, forcing over 60,000 members of the Cherokee Nation to walk "The Trail of Tears" from the eastern seaboard to the Oklahoma territory, John Phillips' father would never have met his mother. John's parents could not have been more dissimilar. His father, Claude Andrew Phillips, was a rigid, unbending, hard-drinking, US Marine Corps career officer. His mother, Edna Gertrude Gains, was a full-blooded Cherokee from Oklahoma with a cross branded on her arm.

"My dad bought a hotel in Okmulgee, Oklahoma, approximately 60 miles south of Tulsa on a Cherokee reservation," John explains. "Indians working in Okmulgee (or any city) had to have a brand on their arm. My mother was branded with a cross. She would come to Okmulgee to work with her mother whose name was Zora.

My grandmother was a famous mystic from Oklahoma. My dad said that the first time he saw her bending over, making a bed, he knew she was his.

"My dad was Irish Catholic and the priest came to him and said, 'I think you'd better watch yourself. You're getting into trouble with the Gains Boys (Edna's five brothers). They are really rough guys. You'd better marry her or leave her alone.' Her parents told her not to be a fool — marry the guy and get out of here.

"So, my father married her. He went into the Marine Corps, and they moved to Parris Island, South Carolina. She wasn't happy, she didn't want to leave the reservation. She wanted to be an Indian — she loved it, the whole style of living there. She went back to the reservation three times, and three times my dad had to come and get her. Her father had to convince her to go back with him. She always told me that she wished she had stayed on the reservation."

On New Year's Eve, 1922, John's sister Rosemary (Rosie) was born. His mother was in her nineteenth year and doted on her newborn. Two years later a brother, Thomas, was added to the family circle. In mid-1935 John's father was promoted to Major and John's mother was pregnant again. She was 31 and Major Phillips 48.

Those living on the eastern seaboard will never forget the Labor Day weekend hurricane of 1935 that swept in from the Atlantic and devastated the region. South Carolina reported killer winds of 125 miles per hour and crashing 20-foot waves. Lives were lost and damage ranged in the millions, which added to the general misery of The Great Depression. John Edmund Andrew Phillips was born during that storm, 30 August 1935, on Parris Island, South Carolina, a portent, some would say, of his life and career.

Before John began school, his family moved to Alexandria, Virginia, near Washington, DC. His sister Rosie would be the first to say that her little brother John was a horrible child — self-centered, selfish, and difficult to control. "John was a monster as a child. He started playing hooky from school in first grade. That sounds kind of dumb, but it's true. He was expelled from first grade for absenteeism (St. Mary's Catholic Academy). My mother never knew anything about it.

"He would be given money to get on the bus and go to school, but he would end up buying some breakfast in downtown Alexandria and then spend the day at the movies. There were three movie houses that had five cent movies all day long. He would come home just at the right time."

Rosemary was thirteen at the time. Although she vividly recalls how John would embarrass her and her friends and seemingly take great delight in doing it, she recognized he was a gifted child. "From about four years on he was a problem to me, but I loved him dearly. I thought he was really smart and was going to be somebody. He was always the leader. If they had a little club, or something, John was always head man, but his behavior — he was incorrigible.

"My brother Tommy and I would take him on the bus to go to the movies in Washington. We would pretend he wasn't with us because he would immediately get up and just start terrorizing the people on the bus — running back and forth yelling and singing. It was like he was really not all there but he was having a good time. Finally the bus driver would demand to know whose child this was. I had to acknowledge that I was in charge. He'd make us get off the bus and we'd wait for the next one. John would do the same thing on the next bus. Sometimes it took us three buses to get from Alexandria to Washington.

"Tommy and I had seen the Dracula and Frankenstein movies when we were very young. I was so frightened by those movies. I used to have terrible nightmares of bats flying in my window. There was a double bill at one of the theaters in the District and Tommy and I decided that we would take John. We were ready to leave if he got upset — he laughed through the whole thing. He ruined it for everybody around because he just thought it was real funny. I couldn't believe his reaction because I was still scared the second time around. But that is the way he was. He was very unpredictable. You didn't know from one minute to the next what he was going to do."

Bill Throckmorton, who married Rosemary, adds to this portrait of John as a child. "Two stories that I can remember give you a flavor of this kid," Throckmorton recounts. "Rosemary's boss was Judge Singleton. He was the head of Western Union Telegraph Service and a very staid guy. Rosemary took John to the office one day and said, 'I'd like you to meet Johnny, my little brother.' Johnny threw his hands up, screamed, and kicked Judge Singleton in the shins, then ran like hell.

"The second story is about the first time I went out with Rosemary.

Her mother and Johnny came along because Mrs Phillips was springing for dinner. I was working at Western Union and didn't have much money. We went to a place in Washington called the Copper Bowl. It was a little restaurant — kind of intimate — very nice and very quiet. We were at a round table and John is sitting there with a glass of ice tea. He was dipping the spoon in the ice tea and flicking it at all of us. I thought, the little bastard should get it. If he were mine, I'd turn him over my knee. Mrs Phillips didn't do a thing. She said, 'Isn't he cute?' I was ready to break his arms. He was what they would now call a hyperactive kid."

Music has always been paramount in John's life and the hold it has on him can be traced back to his parents. Like most parents in the Depression era, they made their own music, and in doing so instilled a love for lyrics and melody at a very early age. "My mother loved honky tonk and my dad had a beautiful Irish tenor voice. He could sing all night and did on many occasions. I would just lie in bed and listen to him in the dark. I love Irish folk music, I love folk music in general, but I love the Irish ballads especially."

When John's father received a medical discharge from the Marines in 1939, war clouds were gathering. When he tried to re-enlist and was turned down, it was a traumatic blow to his self-esteem. He withdrew from the family and started drinking heavily. Bill Throckmorton was still a member of the Phillips' family and saw the tragedy happen. "When the old man found out that he couldn't be a strong Marine Major any more, he kind of deserted the family and himself. Johnny was left without a model. And I certainly wasn't any model for him when Rosemary and I got married."

While John would readily say that he was "the author of his own misfortune," especially during his adult years, boyhood chum Jimmy Shortt is more charitable in his assessment of things. "Early traumas certainly must have played a role in framing John's unconventional attitude towards convention and authority."

In 1942, John's parents enroled him in Linton Hall, a military school, run by nuns, in Manassas, Virginia. He was to spend four unhappy years, in uniform, at the academy. Jimmy Shortt was also a cadet at Linton Hall and vividly recalls one traumatic incident and how John handled it. "I had run away again and they lined everyone up. There was a thousand kids in this school. Each kid had a military type belt with a brass buckle. The nuns made me and this other guy who also kept running away run through the line naked and they all beat us with their belts. John told me later he was the only one who didn't hit me."

Bill Cleary was also a childhood friend of John. That friendship has endured but not without questioning. "When I first met John, I wasn't quite sure what was going on. I think his mother and my mother bumped our strollers together and at that point we started swinging at one another. It just kinda grew from that. We hung out in the same neighborhood, did the same things every other kid does — steal cars, get hub caps, siphon gas. Just normal things any child would do."

Even though Bill Throckmorton was openly irritated by John's unconventional behavior, he was the one who fostered John's musical talents. "It was just one of those things," Throckmorton explains. "I loved to show off my record collection to anybody who came to my house. Johnny became interested — I don't think I interested him. He was interested in lots of different things and he came in and listened to music. I saw that the kid had an interest in music. I had a guitar and I gave it to him. As far as teaching him 'G' chords and 'F' chords, I don't think that I knew them that well then. I only had a few piano lessons. But he was interested enough to stick it out and we talked a lot about music and listened to it. Every time he came over he'd want to hear records. I love music so much I didn't have a problem with that.

"John had some natural musician qualities — liking music and picking things up very quickly. John is a quick read on everything — very bright, extremely bright. You could see that from his earliest days. I had a friend who used to come over to the house every weekend. He would come over and see Johnny and hear the latest about Johnny doing this or Johnny doing that. He said, 'You know that kid is either going to grow up a millionaire or be in jail by the time he's twenty.'

"When you get to the musician side of things, I never thought he knew much about music per se. I think he learned an awful lot along the way. He picked up the genre of his time. There was what I call an explosion of folk music. Anybody could play — pick up a guitar, learn three chords, and you could play. Johnny picked it up. He had fun with it. I think that's where he was best at it. He was having fun all along.

He had fun at a lot of people's expense, but he was always having fun."

John's sister Rosie knew how unhappy he was at home and went out of her way to make him welcome in her home. Rosie knew it was the lure of music that attracted him, and she was pleased to see that it was the means of building a bond between him and his brother-in-law. "My ex-husband was quite a character. He was the not only a union musician, he was a college professor. He played the drums, which was his primary instrument at the time. He also played the piano, guitar and flute — you name it. He could play about any instrument. He also had quite a collection of old jazz records.

"John spent a lot of time with Bill and music. Bill taught him how to play the guitar. Most guitars have six strings, but Bill had this five-string guitar you played like a ukulele and the chording was like a ukulele. John learned on that, then Bill gave him a regular guitar with the case and everything. I was surprised as John was, to tell the truth, because I didn't think John meant that much to him, but apparently he did."

John readily acknowledges his debt to Bill Throckmorton. "Bill was like a beatnik kind of a guy. I guess he must be fifteen years older than me. I just admired him. He played beautifully, he's a great drummer — he taught me how to play guitar."

According to Bill Cleary, John's career as a musician began with street corner singing. If you could sing you were an "in" person. "There wasn't much doing in those days," Cleary recalls. "Everyone was standing around on the corner. You'd hear a song and then you'd start singing it and find some people that could sing and a couple who couldn't. The ones that couldn't you'd hit and get rid of them. Only the good ones stayed around. Eventually there would just be four, six, or eight who could sing. You'd sing at parties, you'd sing on the corner. When you went to a party, you might make a couple of dollars. That's what we used to try to do. We'd also sing at U.S.O. shows and things like that. You'd get a couple of glasses of punch and a Red Cross pin."

John hung around with some hell-raising rowdies who called themselves The Del-Ray Locals. "They'd slash a tire without batting an eye," Cleary explains. "The one redeeming factor was their singing. We sang a lot, we really did, we really sang a lot. There were some really serious singers there. The guys who were so tough were so shy that they wouldn't sing in public. The first few times that we sang in public I actually had bruises on my knees from bumping them together."

When he was thirteen, John's baseball team made it to the second-ever Little League World Series, but he was not allowed to pitch because his coach had caught him shoplifting. In 1954 at age nineteen, after what could only be called a tumultuous education with the Sisters of St. Mary's Catholic School, the nuns at Linton Hall, and the teachers at George Washington High School, John was accepted into the Naval Academy at Annapolis, Maryland. His family, especially Rosie, were proud of this achievement, and to his credit, John made one of the highest grades in the written entrance examination. In typical fashion, John's guile had to be brought into play in order to pass the medical. "When he took the physical, they found out that he was partially color blind. It runs in my family, my daughter is pastel color blind," Rosie recalls. "John went to a special optometrist or someone who trained him how to recognize certain colors even though he didn't see them as colors. He was taught how to distinguish between shades of what he was seeing as green or red or pink . . . He was able, by hook or by crook, to pass the examination to get into the naval academy. It was a very, very, proud day.

"My dad had always said that he had two sons and that he wanted one to be a priest and one to be a bartender. They both had more bartender in them than they did priest. John's going into the naval academy was almost as though he had made Pope. My dad was so proud, so very proud. He was not doing it willingly because other people wanted him to do it more than he wanted to do it. Obviously the family wanted him to do it. His girlfriend, at the time, was very much for him doing it, and she was going to be loyal and faithful and wait for him for four years. John had a great deal of pressure to go in. He finally succumbed."

Not surprisingly, John chafed at the regimentation of the Academy and began talking about getting out. Bill and Rosie did their best to try and talk John into staying, but he wanted out after a year-and-a-half, though he had to do it honorably so it wouldn't reflect adversely on his father. As Bill recalls, "John called and said he was thinking about dropping out. We talked to him and gave him the 'you know you can make it' sort of thing. He called later and said, 'Well, if you two guys can make it, then I guess I can make it. You talked me into it — it's a good deal.' He went for a little longer and then left — he was his own man.

"Johnny would always come to Rosie when things were tough or he needed to talk to somebody. I thought that was great. I don't find it among a lot of brothers and sisters now. He'd always come and ask her for advice — wouldn't always follow it."

In September 1956 John enroled at Hampden-Sydney College with a basketball scholarship, but by October he had been expelled. While the family begrudgingly accepted the fact that he dropped out, they were in no position or mood to underwrite John's new-found freedom, Rosie explains. "My mother and father were not going to give him any more money. He would go out looking for a job and usually ended up being a salesman of some kind. He sold sewing machines. In fact, he became quite proficient on a sewing machine. He sold me a sewing machine. It was one of the first kind that you could use for free embroidery work. He was sewing his name 'John Phillips' all over the place. He also sold cemetery plots. He would tell the poor people that in the state of Virginia if you didn't own a piece of land to be buried in before you die, you would be thrown in the dump. He sold a lot of cemetery plots. Apparently, a lot of money never got back to the company. People died and the family went looking for the plots and there were none. John never got into trouble over that but I think that later he regretted having done that."

Bill Cleary remembers John's career as a cemetery plot salesman and tells a couple of hilarious stories about tarring roofs, trying to maintain a swimming pool, and their after-hours visits to all-black clubs in the District of Columbia while John was working there as a car salesman. "He was working as a cemetery plot salesman, but that got a little difficult and he wanted a change. So he got a job with Virginia Roofing, tarring roofs — he had that job for half-a-day. The temperature on the roof was about a hundred-and-twenty. I had always worked at swimming pools and told John to find a nice pool. There were lots of women around, the water's nice, and there's a lot of fringe benefits. We found a pool for him and Mike Berand, a guy we used to sing with. Problem was they didn't know how to run a pool and would call me every now and then. The worst call was the day that they tried to change the chlorine tank, which is an absolutely killer gas. They forgot to put a washer on the tank. It was leaking and they didn't have any ammonia. The only way you can tell it's really leaking is to put the ammonia up and it starts smoking. I get in my car and I go about a hundred miles an hour. I tell them to get everyone out of the pool. I put on a gas mask, change the tank, and put on the right washer.

"I recall going to a black club in DC. We were the only two white people there. They were passing guns — prostitutes going upstairs. They were all very nice to us because John worked at an automobile dealership at 7th and "O" and we were in there a lot. We'd been to a lot of black neighborhood bars, so they got to know us. They knew we could sing. We'd also go to jazz clubs and after-hours clubs. There wasn't any problem because they had seen us before, but we were actually scared to death while we were in there."

John soon tired of the 9 to 5 world and turned his attention to music. He asked Bill Throckmorton if there was any way he could make a demo, as John recalls. "I told Bill that I wanted to make a record, a demo. He had this band that played every weekend. Bill was just great — he was really a wonderful guy. We got along, we understood each other on an intellectual basis. He said, 'I have this group so if you want to make this demo, come on in.' We went into this small room — very tiny, little space. The first time we ever heard our voices coming back, it was Bill Cleary and I and Jimmy Shortt and somebody else. It was amazing when you hear your voice back through the speaker."

The demo was not vintage John Phillips. Bill Throckmorton has no hesitation about what he thought of the demo. "They were bad. They were really bad. I mean, they missed notes, they couldn't be together, the takes were five, six, seven, eight, and nine. John took it around and tried to peddle it to a lot of people. The piano player and I were looking around for jobs and we went to a local booking agent and he said something about hearing some kids that came in, they were screaming — they were awful. I said, 'What was the name?' And he said, 'The guy's name was Phillips or something.' I said, 'That's the group we played behind.' He said, 'You played with them? You guy's were great! I can use you — *they* were awful."

Tarring roofs and selling cemetery plots certainly wasn't John's idea of gainful employment. Pounding the sidewalks and knocking on doors in New York trying to find work as a musician wasn't his idea of fun either. "First I did it by myself," John recalls. "I had my guitar on my back and I would knock on doors. The people would say, 'Get out of here! You haven't got it.'"

Fate shone on John when he got a job at Manhattan Auto in Washington. "He used to steal a car when he worked for Manhattan Auto," recalls Bill Cleary. "Well, he didn't exactly steal it. He had a demonstrator and was allowed to put twenty miles a day on it. The night he was off we'd jump in that car and put about eight hundred miles on it in two days, going to New York and hustling songs. John would talk to agents and try to get a record label. We had some tapes at that point — beat the hell out of the car."

Phil Blondheim worked at the dealership with John and remembers the day he was fired along with John for 'borrowing' these cars. "John was working at this car dealership, in Washington, and so was I. We just took off without telling our boss, who was probably the best salesman who ever lived. He could close a deal better than any ten salesmen and he was very stone-faced about everything. We didn't report for work for a couple of days, and when we came back, we were sitting in a little coffee shop across the street from the dealership. Our boss walks in and says, 'Oh, hi guys, so you went to New York — songs and stuff?'

"All we could say was, 'Yeah.'

"He says, 'Well you know I really hope you make a lot of money there because you ain't going to make it here.'

"So we were fired."

Phil Blondheim would soon make the same commitment to a career in music that John made, eventually changing his name to Scott McKenzie and performing with John in their band The Journeymen. "I made a decision when I was selling used cars that it was this — or that," John explains. "There was no in-between. I was either going to be a musician or was going to die — you know, I didn't care."

Over the course of the next few years, John Phillips would launch a successful career as a folk artist, forming three bands — The Abstracts, The Smoothies, and The Journeymen — before meeting three aspiring musicians who were as unconventional, precocious, and talented as he was. With Michelle Gilliam, Cass Elliot, and Denny Doherty, he would create The Mamas and The Papas.

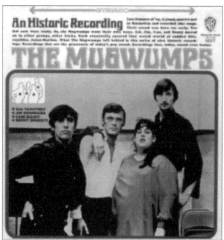

Before they became known as
The Mamas and The Papas they called
themselves The Magic Circle, the title
of a CD released in 1999 including
music from their earlier bands,
The Big Three, The Halifax Three,
The Mugwumps, The Smoothies,
The Journeymen, and The New
Journeymen (shown above).

The Mamas and The Papas performing live in their signature hippie attire.
(Photo by Guy Webster)

THE MAMAS & THE PAPAS

CREEQUE ALLEY

Creeque Alley

John and Michie were gettin' kind of itchie
*   just to leave the folk music behind*
Zal and Denny workin' for a penny,
*   tryin' to get a fish on the line;*
In the coffeehouse Sebastian sat,
*   and after every number they passed the hat.*
McGuinn and McGuire just gettin' higher in L.A.,
*   you know where it's at;*
And no one's gettin' fat except Mama Cass . . .

When Cass was a sophomore, planned to go to Swarthmore,
*   But she changed her mind one day;*
Standin' on the turnpike, thumb out to hitchhike:
*   take me to New York right away.*
When Denny met Cass he gave her love bumps,
*   called John and Zal and that was the Mugwumps.*
McGuinn and McGuire couldn't get no higher
*   but that's what they were aimin' at;*
And no one's gettin' fat except Mama Cass . . .

(John Phillips and Michelle Phillips, ASCAP)

During the mid-1950s, Susan Adams, an aspiring ballerina and a direct descendant of President John Adams, caught the eye of John Phillips, and they were married by a Justice of the Peace in Arlington, Virginia in May 1957. John gave the J.P. a check for $25.00 — it bounced. "Susie" was pregnant and Jeffrey Phillips was born on 13 December 1957. But family responsibilities of fatherhood were not sufficient to hold John down, a wanderlust he attributes to his native heritage. As he explains, he ventured with a friend to Cuba during the revolution without ever telling Susie that he was going. It was a heady time for mercenaries and soldiers of fortune; even film star Errol Flynn went to Cuba to lend his support to Fidel Castro and his revolution. "I hear the drums," John tries to explain. "It means I'm not careful. Obviously in my life people know I'm not careful. The Indian part was really hearing the drums. People shouldn't bother me. I'm quick off the mark. It's just the way I am. I can't help it.

"That was sort of an ill-fated trip, actually. We were all inspired freedom fighters and this was before Castro had gone communist. They (Castro's army) were fighting in the hills. They were closer to Havana than we thought they were.

"I told Susie that my friend Mike Johnson needed some luggage because Mike was going on a trip. Actually, I packed it full of my own stuff and left the house. I think I sent her a postcard from Cuba."

Years later when Susie thinks about John's unannounced and sudden departure for Cuba, she has a wry smile, but it wasn't funny at the time. She was left to fend for herself and their son. From the way she describes it she still hasn't forgiven John. "That bastard! I had two beautiful steaks which I had marinated. We seldom could afford steak. John came in with this guy and said, 'Susie I need to borrow a suitcase because so-and-so's father died.' I said sure, fine. They went into the bedroom, closed the door and packed the suitcase. John said, 'I'm going to take him to the airport. I'll see you in about an hour.' One hour, two hours, three hours. I thought, that son-of-a-bitch packed his clothes."

John's vision of being one of Castro's inspired freedom fighters was more fantasy than reality. "All Mike Johnson and I had with us was a box full of 45's. Mike was the sort of guy who made jokes — deadly jokes. As we were getting off the plane, his suitcase weighed about five hundred pounds, like it was full of ammunition, or something. We had about five hundred singles, and when we got to customs they made us play all the records and listen to them. They were looking for hidden messages, coded words and things. We were being interrogated at the airport in a foreign language. We had no idea of what they were talking about. We were just trying to pigeon talk our way through it. So finally they said, okay, get in this car. It was an old Buick. We jumped in the back and thought we were going straight to the tombs.

"We got about fifteen minutes from the airport and he said, 'Where do you want to go?'"

"'What do you mean? Where do you want to go?'"

"We thought we were under arrest. I didn't know.

"'Where's a nice hotel?'"

"He asked how much money we had and we said, 'None.' He took us to this place and came back the next morning. He said he was going to smuggle us out. The city was cordoned off by troops. I don't think he had any intention of smuggling us out of Havana, 'cause what money he could make for a risk of life, limb, and property to get us through wasn't quite worth it. We never got out of the city of Havana.

"Every morning we went out for breakfast at this small little area in front of a night club. We'd start drinking rum and Coca Cola — real Yankees. They started showing dirty movies and things like that. The next thing we knew the sun was going down and we'd missed another day of the revolution. This went on for weeks. Suddenly it was just impossible to get out of the city. We played our guitars. We weren't very good guitarists but at least we were Americans who played rock'n'roll or country and western. Everly Brothers. Things like that. We were playing on the corner four or five days, four or five hours every day, and collected enough money to live on and pay our hotel bill.

"One day a guy comes up to us and says, 'Would you like to be on television?'"

"'Yeah, that would be great.'"

"'Come with me.'"

"We thought we were going for an audition or something . . . or to meet the producers of the show. We get there and the guy says, 'I have two Americans who sing Everly Brothers songs, folk music and rock. Do you want to use them?'"

"'Yeah! Have them ready in ten minutes.'"

"So ten minutes later we were on Cuban television dressed exactly as we were — it was rag tag. Then things really started popping — like people walking on the streets with bottles of rum, whisky, and beer in their hands, grenades going off with tanks going by. It was a lark, at first, then it became very serious. There was a diminishing number of planes leaving for Key West. As the hours went by it was time for Americans to get out.

"I had fallen in love with this hooker. Her name was Sandy. I was saving all my pennies . . . I finally got the money together. She was working in a club so we went to her room and made mad passionate love over a bottle of rum all night long. In the morning she wouldn't even take the money. I was really discouraged because I wasn't even good enough to get paid for."

Revenge is sweet but it is sweeter when it is two-fold, as Susie remembers, with relish. "John wrote a check to the airlines (for the tickets to Cuba) and I refused to cover the check 'cause we didn't have the money — the check bounced. I think he arrived in Cuba with like ten bucks, so it was ten bucks worth of fun. When he came back he really had to eat crow — he really did!"

Despite the amount of crow he had to eat, John soon after headed out to Los Angeles, where he performed solo at a number of clubs before returning home to celebrate Jeffrey's first birthday in December 1958. Early the next year he teamed up with Phil Blondheim, Bill Cleary, and Mike Boran and put together The Abstracts. Phil recalls how John worked on arranging the members of the band. "The first time I met John it was at a party, in his apartment, that lasted about two weeks. He was sitting on the floor playing the guitar. I said, 'What are you doing?

"'I don't know, I write songs.'

"'Geez, I want to be a singer.'

"'Okay, sit down.'

"He immediately gave me a harmony part to a song and it was pure chemistry. That's what John does with everybody — just hands out harmony parts.

"The groups that really influenced John and me the most were The Four Freshmen and The Hi Lo's, also The Modernaires (with Paula Kelly). The Modernaires were one of the only groups, at that time, who used both men and women equally. It wasn't like one lead singer, with the women doing 'do wop, do wop' in the background.

"What influenced us in a pop vein were The Four Lads. The main reason for that was because Bill Cleary had this magnificent bell-toned voice that at least sounded as good, if not better, than the tenor in The Four Lads. We just tried to listen to as many of those albums as we could and tried to mimic the sound and do those voicings. John was always as much of a vocal arranger as he was a song writer. He was more of a vocal arranger in the beginning."

The lush harmonies that set The Mamas and The Papas apart from other contemporary groups can be traced back to The Abstracts and the influence of the smooth singing groups who were so popular when John was getting his musical feet wet. "I was very influenced by the Hi Lo's and by The Four Freshmen," John concurs. "They really were my life — I loved them. I wanted those harmonies, so we got a guy named George Wilkins to do the arrangements. They were very difficult to learn, like a tone apart, really difficult harmonies. That was the birth of The Abstracts. George really worked on us and believed in us."

There is nothing more competitive than the music business, and, talent notwithstanding, it takes the unique skills of a booking agent who has contacts to get a group or solo act before the public. John and The Abstracts were fortunate that George Wilkins knew New York booking agent Charlie Ryan and made a strong recommendation on behalf of both of them in 1960. "I met George Wilkins because he started a recording studio and recommended us to The Four Abstracts," Ryan recalls. "They were doing rock and roll. Here you've got four guys that didn't rock and roll, they just didn't look rock and roll. You got tall Johnny Phillips, and the others — they just didn't look the part — but they had some great songs. I called a contact at Decca Records and told him what I thought of the group. 'These fellows have got talent. Not only do they have songs, they have original songs. They are worth a try.'

"I took the boys up and they auditioned. We put them on Decca Records. To make a long story short, that didn't go so good. Their records should have sold like hot cakes, but they weren't even selling like pancakes. I said to John that what we should do is go to a different field — maybe go folk rock. They recorded four great songs. I can think of three of them — *Ride, Ride, Ride, Lonely Boy and Pretty Girl*, and a tremendous arrangement on *Michael Row the Boat*. I mean tremendous. It was never released but it was great. When we finished the date, I thought we had a hit with *Lonely Boy and Pretty Girl*, but it wasn't to be."

Bill Cleary is still grateful that Charlie Ryan went all out to help the group make ends meet, including booking photo sessions for magazines. It wasn't art but it helped pay the rent. "Charlie Ryan was a great ol' guy. He used to get us jobs modeling for *True Confession* and *True Romance* magazines. It paid pretty well — about forty bucks an hour and you'd just do these shots. I think John was a cadaver one time. I've forgotten what I was."

John chuckles at the thought of modeling a corpse. If fate hadn't intervened, a few years down the road he could very well have been rehearsing for destiny. "I was always the corpse, Scott (a.k.a. Phil Blondheim) was always the lover. I'd be lying on the floor, I'd be murdered, I'd be climbing out a window, or something. Scott would be making love to a beautiful woman. I guess in the end it always worked out that way. It was pretty strange. I was always dead. I was always lying on the floor. I never moved."

By the time The Abstracts tasted their first success, John had become the father of Laura MacKenzie Phillips, born 10 November 1959. When Phil Blondheim decided to assume the stage name Scott McKenzie, he took the surname, with a slight change in the spelling, from John's daughter's middle name. Despite his wanderlust, Susie encouraged John in his career as a musician, working menial jobs to save money and making certain the group looked presentable on stage. She was genuinely pleased for him. "I fell in love with him because he was a literal genius," she declares, "an unbelievable talent. He would cop somebody's tie and one of the local guys would say, 'Hey, you're wearing my tie. Where the hell did you get that?' And John would cop a shirt because he never really cared about clothes, he really didn't. Just give him his music.

"I was with him when he was with The Abstracts. I really loved it because I was able to go to their shows and Rosie would babysit. I would dress them, press their pants, and polish their shoes. One night I noticed when John was performing that he had one navy blue sock on and one black sock on. The stage was raised and said to myself, 'Oh shit, how did I do that?' I enjoyed it."

In the late 1950s and early '60s the Elmwood Casino in Windsor, Ontario was one of the top clubs in North America. Many of the established stars of the age like Sophie Tucker and Jimmy Durante played there to full houses. Charlie Ryan booked The Abstracts for a month over Christmas in 1959, as Bill Cleary recalls. "We had a suite at one end and a suite at the other end. They had eight or ten chorus girls in between. You always had someone to have lunch and dinner with. It made it pretty nice — it made it pretty convenient."

Charlie Ryan remembers the problem he had with the name of the band. "The Abstracts" simply was not a memorable name. "What happened in those days when you weren't a name was they'd take advantage of you and make you do anything they wanted 'cause you were there. Maybe there was a choreographer who decided to make them Mounties at the finish of a production number, but they did their act before that. All of a sudden the group said they had to have a new name. We should have called them The Grand Funk. I said many times we could have called them this and that. I'd be riding with my daughter in the car and I'd be listening to Alan Freed. He'd say, 'Now here they come The Four . . . .' So I said to my daughter, you're going to see the day when they say, 'Here come The Four Fucks. . . .' Now we couldn't call them that. But that was the way they were coming up with names. I didn't know what to call them, so one day I said, 'I'll call them The Smoothies.' I was sorry I ever said that, but we couldn't think of a name."

The Abstracts did change their name to The Smoothies, and one of John's songs, which they recorded as a single, *Softly*, got enough radio play to convince Dick Clark to book them for his show *American Bandstand* in July 1960. Dick Clark is still asked about The Mamas and The Papas. "People are always saying to me, when was the first time that I remember The Mamas and The Papas, or saw them, or met John Phillips. The truth is I don't remember the first time I ever saw John. But the last time I worked with him he asked me if I remembered a group The Smoothies? 'No!' I said. He told me that they appeared on the show in the very early '60s. They did a song called *Softly*. They were all so scared that nobody wanted to do the lip sync. They finally told Scott McKenzie to do it. He did the whole thing with his eyes closed and his fists clenched."

Dick Clark might have had problems remembering The Smoothies' appearance on his show, but John certainly does with humorous overtones. "The funny thing is, we were so folk orientated in Greenwich Village that we didn't really know what *American Bandstand* was. Conway Twitty showed up. Conway was great. We were so square. Conway was like 'Hey, what's going on!' He'd take his coat off and throw it in the corner. Someone would catch it. He had four bodyguards and this huge black limo — we were in a yellow taxi. It was so different. We weren't oriented to all that. Suddenly things started moving, clicking. We were having lots of fun and stuff. It was something really new to us."

Although they recorded an album, the band nevertheless broke up during Christmas 1960, with John and Scott wanting to try The Greenwich Village scene, soon forming a band called The Journeymen with Dick Weissman, a dazzling folk instrumentalist whose musicianship on the banjo complemented John's songwriting and rhythm guitar and Scott's velvet-smooth vocals and beautifully controlled harmonies. The Journeymen barnstormed the campus and folk circuit and quickly built a following with their quality music. In March 1961, they signed with Weber-Cardenas, a management group, and then signed a recording contract with Capitol Records. In April they appeared at Gerdes Folk City in The Village, sharing a bill with Bob Dylan, who was performing his first paid gig.

The Journeymen were booked into the Hungry i in San Francisco for a month during 1961, at a time when the music scene in San Francisco had not yet flowered, as singer-songwriter Hoyt Axton recalls. Axton is the son of Mae Boren Axton who composed one of Elvis Presley's greatest hits, *Heartbreak Hotel*, and he would write such diverse songs as *The Pusher*, recorded by Steppenwolf, and *Joy To The World*, recorded by Three Dog Night, both on Dunhill Records, the label that would also sign The Mamas and The Papas. "John and I first met in a club in San Francisco back in 1959," Axton recounts. "I used to sing in the joint for tips. I'd make about eight or ten dollars a night and was glad to have it. My rent was only six bucks a month so it didn't matter that much.

"San Francisco was great! It was basketball in the streets at night. It was wonderful. There were people walking down the street, drinking cold beers, and not being hassled. There were people sleeping on benches, underneath park benches and under bushes — and not being kicked around by the cops. Nobody was throwing them in jail for not having any money. It was a great time. You didn't have to have any money to be part of what was happening. What was happening was some basic organic beginning of a movement that ended up in that whole flower generation. Those beginnings were in the late '50s and early '60s in San Francisco.

"It started in the North Beach area. There were a lot of us musicians hanging out there, a lot of neat people — days of wine and roses. Sure the wine was cheap and the roses were stolen, but what the hell?"

While performing at The Hungry i in this hedonistic atmosphere, John Phillips met Michelle Gilliam. Michelle Holly was born to Gil and Joyce Gilliam on 4 June 1944 in the waiting room of the Seaside Memorial Hospital in Long Beach, California. Following a stint in the merchant marines early in World War II, Michelle's father met her mother in 1940 when he was a production assistant working on the movie set of *North West Mounted Police*, starring Gary Cooper and Paulette Goddard. Her mother was the accountant on the picture. Following her mother's death as a result of sub-acute endocarditis, Michelle's devastated father embarked upon a nomadic existence with his young daughters. Michelle and her sister Russell Ann, who was a year older, moved from California to New York to Mexico for six years and back to California.

By the time Michelle was back in Los Angeles and enroled in Marshall High School, she was playing cello in the junior orchestra and being noticed by the boys. She was quickly becoming a raving beauty. She was still in her mid-teens when she caught John's eye in San Francisco's Hungry i and ultimately became his lover, wife, and a founding Mama in The Mamas and The Papas.

For the Hungry i engagement, John and Susie had decided to move to the San Francisco area, taking an apartment in Sausalito. "John made arrangements for Susie and the two children to fly to California," his sister Rosie explains. "They got an apartment in

Sausalito and he would go to work (at the Hungry i) and then come back home. Susie and I both thought, 'Oh! this is really going to make the marriage — everything is going to work out alright.' She was delirious that he had asked her to come to California."

Even though she was delirious about the move, Susie had misgivings. "The Journeymen were fine, I thought they were great until I discovered that John was seeing just about everybody. John always had a woman, he still has, I can betcha a million bucks on that. The move was an emotional thing for me because, although I'd been to Europe and had traveled quite a bit, it was an entirely different move in that we were moving en masse — with what little we had we were moving en masse. I felt kind of hesitant about moving some place with John as sole support. I knew in the back of my mind that it wasn't going to work. I did it because I loved him. It was probably good that I did it, very selfishly, because at that point Michelle came into the picture.

"I don't think that we had been in Mill Valley more than three months when little miss teenie bopper meandered into the Hungry i. I had really seen her before John saw her because I was at the Hungry i and thought, 'Who is that?' She was all in black — black coat, black dress, black shoes. At sixteen years old, made up like a china doll. If I had done that, my mother would have whipped me around the corner."

It didn't take Rosie long to spot potential trouble. "This gorgeous young blond was hanging around the bar and I really mean really gorgeous — she's gorgeous today. Michelle fell madly in love with John and decided that this was the man she wanted — she got him."

John is quite candid in his account of meeting Michelle. "That story has a very dark side — and light side — actually. Michelle was the typical Californian that Brian Wilson used to write about. She was one of the very first runaways — it was one of her claims to fame. She ran away and moved to San Francisco to live with a friend of hers, Tamar Udall, who her father used to date, and moved in with her. Tamar knew the fellow who did portraits and caricatures in the lobby of the Hungry i, which was a very hip, North Beach, nightclub. It's now a parking lot. We played there for about six months and were managed by the same person who managed The Kingston Trio — Frank Weber. We opened for Lenny Bruce, Shelley Berman, Dick Gregory, and an endless number of people.

"Michelle came there with her friend. She was absolutely beautiful — very, very, appealing. I was married, twenty-five years old and had two children. She was sixteen. It was like one of those sad stories . . . I guess."

As Michelle tells the story of their meeting, "I was seventeen when I went to San Francisco for the summer. While there we decided to go see Dick Gregory at the Hungry i. We got there a little late and the first act was on and that was The Journeymen. I remember that I was completely taken by the sound of the group, but I was really taken by the tall guitar player who was obviously leader of the group. After the show we asked Enrico Banducci, the owner of the club, if he would introduce us to the guys, which was as easy to do then as it probably is now.

"So we were introduced to John, Scott, and Dick. Later on that night we ran into Scott at Enrico's restaurant. He and my girlfriend started to see each other on a regular basis. That's how I started to see John."

John takes up the story from here. "She was very aggressive about the whole thing. I really wasn't looking for a new love or new affair. The Journeymen went to places around the San Francisco area, playing different night clubs. She would show up with Tamar. She finally just wore my resistance down. I really had no intention of it ever ending up being a life-long situation — she seemed to have every intention."

John might have thought it was just another transient affair but Michelle had her own agenda. "I knew that John was married. But I also had the feeling that he was unhappily married — that he was married because of his two children and, you know, when you are seventeen you really believe what you want to believe. At the beginning of the relationship I really felt that it was just a matter of time before he would break up his marriage and I would be there.

"It was late July when I met John and I would say that probably by the end of October I had gone to see Susie. I thought at that time my relationship with John was really over. He had kind of disappeared — gone on the road. I hadn't heard from him for two or three weeks, and when you are seventeen, that feels like a very long time. I didn't really intend to see Susie. I was just curious about where they lived. This friend and I went to the address and he offered to go upstairs and pretend like he is an encyclopedia salesman so that he could get to meet her and then tell me what she was like. He went up there and came back down and we left.

"'So how did it go?'

"'Well, I broke down and I told her that I was actually a friend of yours and she said that she'd really like to meet you.'

"'Turn the car around . . . let's go meet her!'

"I went back and saw her. She asked if she could make me a tuna sandwich and she did. She was very sweet and tried to dissuade me from seeing John again. She told me that John had a Michelle in every town and that I would only be hurt by him if I intended to prolong the affair any longer. I was really prepared for it to be over, but a week or two after that meeting, John showed up at the door and it started again."

Although John emphatically denies Susie's allegations that he had a "Michelle in every city and this kind of thing," he did confess to Susie that he had fallen in love with Michelle. "I fell in love with her. It was just that simple. Susie said, 'You're in love with her, aren't you?'

"'Yeah! I think I am.'

"About two days later Susie took the kids, the car, the furniture and a U-haul and headed back East again."

John is enough of a pragmatist to know that even though Michelle and Susie still speak, too much has happened for them to ever become close. "They ended up being good friends and they still talk to each other quite a bit. I think it is sort of surface. I don't think they really have a bonding."

Susie and John legally separated in April 1962, and two weeks later Michelle joined John when The Journeymen opened in Juarez, Mexico, where he arranged a Mexican divorce from Susie. John and Michelle were married by a Justice of The Peace in Rockland, Maryland on 31 December 1962. Scott McKenzie was John's best man.

During those months in San Francisco, John began writing songs with John Stewart of The Kingston Trio. "John was the only one I found I could ever write with," John Stewart explains. "He was incredibly easy to write with. We wrote a song called *Chilly Winds* that has remained one of The Kingston Trio's standbys. We stayed up all night and wrote something like fifty-two verses to the song. *Oh Miss Mary* was a song that I came up with and we went out in a row boat, on the Sausalito Bay, and wrote the song."

The Journeymen cut their second album in Minneapolis, Minnesota in mid-April 1962 and were booked to play The Shadows in Washington, DC, in July. Heavy bookings, well into the fall, plus jingles for Schlitz Beer and American Express, kept the band busy. At Easter 1963 Dick Weissman left the band to write serious folk music; nevertheless, the band continued to experience success, performing as the opening act at Washington DC's Shoreham Hotel for Bill Cosby and releasing NEW DIRECTIONS IN FOLK MUSIC, their third album. The Journeymen were booked to appear on ABC's top-rated *Hootenanny Show* with Johnny Cash and Judy Collins, which resulted in the band becoming part of the Hootenanny Tour with Glenn Yarborough of The Limelighters and a Canadian group calling themselves The Halifax Three, featuring future Papa, Denny Doherty.

Dennis "Denny" Doherty was born in Halifax, Nova Scotia on 29 November 1941, one of five children born to Irish-Canadian parents Marie and Dennis Doherty. He has a brother Joseph and three sisters — Francis, Joan, and Denise. Although he dropped out of high school in grade 9, he began his singing career at an early age in the glee club at St. Patrick's High School. In 1957 he started singing with a local Halifax band called The Hipsters. The following year he earned regular money as a pawn broker in Halifax, all the while singing at weddings and bar mitzvahs to make extra money and hone his skills. He became a member of The Colonials before moving to New York and changing the name to The Halifax Three. He soon became part of The Village and hootenanny scene, where he teamed up with fellow Canadian Zal Yanovsky, Jim Hendricks, John Sebastian, and future Mama Cass Elliot to form the Mugwumps. Yanovsky and Sebastian would go on to form The Lovin' Spoonful.

Denny recalls his early years as a singer. "As a boy I started singing for insurance salesmen. On a dare I got up and sang at the local hockey rink. Me and the boys used to drive around in a '52 Ford. The boys in the back seat could imbibe. A couple of the guys and myself would sing along with the radio and the people in the front would turn around and tell us to shut up. If you want to sing, go up to the forum and sing — so one night I did. Nobody threw anything. They just sort of stopped dancing and turned around — I was sixteen years old.

"I was in the glee club in St. Patrick's High School (led by Sister Pious). I was singing *Love Me Tender*, and she said, 'Oh! That's an old English folk song.'

"'No! It's Presley down at the Paramount. It's called *Love Me Tender*.'

"'Get out of here! You said that name, the 'E' name.'

"So, I was thrown out of the glee club and didn't think I could sing.

"In '56 I started singing and then was in a band called The Hipsters while I was a pawn broker. Halifax is the east coast command of the Canadian Navy and there were twenty-thousand sailors there at the time. There was only one pawn shop in town and they were coming home with things from all over the world. I worked in the pawn shop and was singing on the weekends at weddings, bar mitzvahs, and that kind of thing.

"We left Halifax as the Colonials, and when we got to New York they asked us what the name of the group was and we said, 'The Colonials.'

"'No! We don't want anything to do with the colonies. Where are you from?'

"'Halifax.'

"'We'll call you The Dorey Men, The Oarlocks . . . where did you say you were from?'

"'Halifax.'

"'The Halifax Three.'

For John, three things stand out in his memory from that November 1962 Hootenanny Tour: he heard Denny Doherty sing, he was on the bus when President Kennedy was shot, and he witnessed racial unrest in the deep South. "One night I decided to catch his act. They were called The Halifax Three. I heard this voice. I've only heard three voices in my life that really meant something to me — Bill Cleary, Scott McKenzie, and Denny Doherty."

Scott McKenzie paints a vivid recollection of the racial unrest the tour faced in the deep South. "We really weren't that famous, but we were somewhat known for our TV exposure when we went on tour. We were in this bus that had 'Hootenanny Show' on it. We were with Glenn Yarborough, from The Limelighters — a wonderful man, a great singer — and a group called The Halifax Three with Denny Doherty. That's when we first met him. Denny swears to this day that I made a sign and hung it on the side of the bus saying 'Ban the Bomb', but I have no memory of that whatsoever. We got to Memphis and Glenn got a phone call from the leaders of CORE, an activist committee. They wanted to talk to everybody. They were in Mississippi and they knew our next stop was Jackson, Mississippi. They asked us if we'd meet them at the Jackson Airport. Glenn, John, and I met them in this conference room. . . . It was the first time that I ever realized that I was under surveillance, or anything, by plain clothes men. They were asking us not to perform that night at the Civic Auditorium because there was a local statute, at that time, that if it was a white event any black person being caught within a block would probably be charged with disturbing the peace, even though Jackson was technically desegregated.

"This put us in somewhat of a quandary. It was like being forced up against the wall and saying okay, are you going to take a position or are you going to cop out. What are you going to do?

"We went to this school, a very small university, and that's the first time I ever saw anything like the outline of a burnt cross. It was very mixed, racially, there were a lot of black and white people. The Dean had this huge bandage on his jaw. Somebody had knocked a hole in it. He had tried to go to church the Sunday before, the congregation was mixed, some white, some black — they all had been beaten up.

"It started really coming home to us. They were asking us to perform in the chapel and refuse to perform at the auditorium as a matter of protest. We wanted to but we were under contract with the promoter for three or four concerts. He had put up an advance and we were literally in the position where nobody had the money if he chose to sue us. John had to get on the phone a lot to our manager in New York. They had the wires tapped so they heard these conversations. Some representative of a town official visited the promoter and said, 'Look let them do this — don't sue them — the last thing the town wants is publicity.'

"So we did it. We performed in this chapel, on campus. Outside there were students with walkie talkies. It was a very dark night. They were afraid of being visited by night riders of the Ku Klux Klan. Apparently, the local law enforcement agencies had told the Klan — hands off! But we had to get out-of-town that night. That was the deal. We ended up being the first group of entertainers ever to honor the CORE's request not to perform. Overnight we became heros to some people and villains to others."

Like most other North Americans, Denny Doherty vividly recalls where he was on 23 November 1963. "We were about forty miles outside Dallas. We were stopped for sodas and refueling the bus and heard on the radio that President Kennedy had been shot. After that everything got very 'waffley' and the tour sort of finished on a blah.

"I went to Hollywood with the group to see if we could coerce the road manager into doing something, anything, with us in L.A. — nothing happened. Our guitar player, 'Soro' Sornonski, and I went back to Washington, DC. We waited on tables and tended bar in a beer joint in Georgetown called Max Pipe and Drum.

"In the meantime The Big Three was performing — Cass Elliot, Tim Rose, and Jim Hendricks. They were on a bus tour when folk music disappeared — commercial folk music, as such, that you could make a living at. I don't know where it went. Folk music went electric because we went electric. This gets kind of confusing, at this point, because everybody was sort of in flux.

"I came back to Washington and got together with Cass and Jim Hendricks and we formed a group called The Mugwumps. At first it was Cass Elliot and The Big Three, which was Soro, myself, John Sebastian, and Jim Hendricks. Art Stokes was our drummer — good drummer.

"We went electric and went back to Washington where our managers owned a club called The Shadows. They put us in there and gave us fifty bucks a week, each, and an apartment over in Arlington. We could eat steaks at the club and had a car to drive. Then it was, Hello! Rock'n'Roll. I'd been in rock'n'roll in 1957 with the Hipsters in Halifax, so it was an easy transition to make."

In Denny Doherty, John Phillips found the perfect male lead vocalist and front man for his bands, as John explains. "I had to have him. I'm sort of a background guy. I don't like to sing lead. I like to write songs. I like to do arrangements, tell the band what to do — mix and stuff. I'm not crazy about standing up front. Denny just had this velvet, liquid, voice. It was insane to me, someone like Bing Crosby, so good and still is. Denny is one of the great singers of the entire world."

Denny recalls being invited to dinner by John and Michelle, where he was asked to join The New Journeymen. "I got a call from John who remembered me from the road. Scott McKenzie had left the group The New Journeymen and Marshall Brickman wanted to get out. He wanted to go write and do whatever he wanted to do. John and Michelle invited me over to dinner one night to get together and sing because they had some more bookings to finish as The New Journeymen. I had dinner and we sat up until about four in the morning singing all kinds of songs.

"'We are going to Washington!'

"'What are you talking about, John?'

"'We have a booking at the Shoreham Hotel for two weeks — it starts in three days.'"(They were to open for Bill Cosby over Christmas 1964.) And so Denny became a member of The New Journeymen and a founding member of The Mamas and The Papas.

Michelle remembers that night as well. "I remember the night. We started singing together and working out some songs. Boy! It was incredible singing with Denny because Denny had a voice where John and I didn't really have great lead voices — neither did Marshall for that matter. Denny had a voice and all of a sudden we were working with someone who could really sing — that was a whole revelation for us."

Denny wasn't too thrilled when John told him what he had to do before they left for Washington, though. When you consider John's appearance during The Mamas and The Papas years, it was a strange request. "I was pretty naive. I was still very folk. My hair was short. Denny's hair was long," John explains.

"'You'll have to cut your hair.'

"'I'll have to cut my hair?'

"He hated to do it, but Denny cut his hair."

The hair was one thing but learning the songs in such a short time was another hurdle for Denny, as he recalls.

"'Three days? I don't know any of the songs.'

"'We'll learn them,' said John, 'we'll learn them.'

"Twenty-eight songs, three days later, twenty-four hours a day. We got to know the local chemist very well which kept us up for three days learning all those songs. I thought that the way I had learned them I was going right out of my head, but we kept it together. This was like Thursday, Friday, Saturday, Sunday and go to Washington and open. We did that gig, then several other concerts. We had about eight, nine, ten thousand dollars and an American Express card."

In 1964 The Beatles had just come out with their first album. Denny really loved them, though John wasn't that impressed at first. Denny convinced him otherwise, while encouraging him to write similar kinds of songs. "We took some acid," John recalls, "and Denny put on a Beatles album and a pair of headphones on me.

"'I want you to listen to this, over and over, again.'

"I must have listened to it for twelve hours.

"'Okay, I know the whole album.'

"I memorized every twist and turn of the whole thing.

"Then Denny said, 'Now write a lot of songs like those.'

"'Okay, fine.'

"So that's what I did. I just started writing songs and took a mind bend in that direction. I became a pop song writer all of a sudden." That The Mamas and The Papas would soon challenge The Beatles for the top of the pop charts was something neither John nor Denny could imagine at the time.

That year John and Michelle moved to New York and rented an apartment on the Upper East Side of Manhattan. Charlie Ryan found work for Michelle while The Journeymen were on the road. "Charlie Ryan kept everybody working," Michelle recalls. "His thing was that everybody should have a job of some sort. When I got there Charlie started sending me out to the rag magazines — *True Love, True Detective*. It was a way to make some easy bucks between jobs. I actually did a cover of *True Detective*. When John would go on the road, he would put me in the Rehearsal Club, which was a home for teenagers who worked in New York — professional models, professional, actors, professional skaters, etc. I don't know who they thought he was, come to think of it. I had to be home at nine or ten o'clock. When he was on the road, he was secure in the knowledge that I had a very structured existence in New York.

"John and I were going through the Holland Tunnel one night when he asked me if I would consider joining a group — his group. The Journeymen had fallen apart and he wanted to put together a new group — The New Journeymen. I told him I had just been offered a seven-hundred dollar a week contract. 'But, we'll be together on the road and you'll make more money than that.' Based on that I decided to get into singing."

During a winter snow storm in 1963, John and Michelle wrote their signature song, *California Dreamin'.* "We were living off Washington Square, in Greenwich Village, and it happened on a Saturday morning," John explains. "Michelle had never seen snow in her entire life and had never been cold. She had lived in Southern California all her life where it never rains. We went for a walk 'cause she had awakened me and said, 'Look out the window, it's amazing!'

"It was just a big New York snowfall. It must have snowed like two or three feet that day. She could not believe that this was coming out of the sky. It was the first time in nineteen years, on this planet, that she had seen this occurrence.

"'I want to go out and walk in it.'

"So, we went out and walked in it. All she had were California clothes and a pair of loafers. The song *California Dreamin'* very much sticks to what we actually did that day. We walked for a while, stopped into a church to get warm, not to pray. She kept talking about California and how much she missed it, all day long.

"I woke up in the middle of the night. I had one of those infamous dreams — the words 'California Dreamin'' kept going through my mind. I started writing some chords for the song and things that I thought fit the melancholy of the song. California was a never-never land for people of the East Coast at the time. We were having one of the toughest winters of all times. You would see people surfing in California on the news."

Besides not thinking she had any talent for songwriting, Michelle was less than thrilled to be wakened out of a sound sleep. "John was always trying to get me to write. It didn't really come very naturally to me, but he did wake me up in the middle of the night. He had his guitar strapped to him and said, 'Listen to this.' He sang me the first verse of *California Dreamin'*.

All the leaves are brown and the sky is gray
I've been for a walk on a winter's day
I'd be safe and warm if I was in LA.
California dreamin' on such a winter's day . . .

"'John, that's pretty.'

"'Get up and help me write it.'

"'I'll help you write it tomorrow.'

"'No. Come on! Help me write it now. You'll thank me for this someday.'

"So I got up and wrote it. I still like to thank him for it. (John and Michelle are listed as co-authors of the song). It's been a great little piece of publishing revenue."

If John and Michelle were in total agreement about the quality of Denny's voice, Denny was even more enthusiastic about Cass Elliot's vocal talent. "You could hear the sound from the street because Monday night at the Bitter End was hootenanny night," Denny recalls. "Anybody who wanted could get up and sing. Usually, it was jammed to the back. If you were performing, you had to wait and get in the shoe box they called a dressing room.

"From the street you could hear the sound . . . 'What in hell was that?'

"'It's The Big Three.'

"'Who is that?'

"'It's Cass! Cass! Cass!'

"The first thing I ever knew about Cass was hearing this voice — and this sound that the trio was making — it was incredible.

"Cass was an Anglophile of the first order. She loved anything British, especially English. She heard that there were two guys in The Halifax Three who were Canadians, me and Zal Yanovsky, and all she wanted to do was talk and blah, blah. One thing led to another. When Cass wanted something she went after it — she was after me for a long time.

"We were all working Bleeker Street — everybody was working Bleeker Street at that point. Dick Cavett was doing standup,

Woody Allen was doing standup, Joan Rivers was with a group called Jim, Jake and Joan doing standup. Bill Cosby was around the corner doing standup. Everybody was there.

"Cass and me got to be drinking buddies. We'd go to The Dugout to drink ourselves under the table, sitting under the table. Cass and I on the floor drinking beers and boilermakers. Girl after my own heart. We just became very good friends."

Cass Elliot was born Naomi Ellen Cohen on 19 September 1941 to Bess and Philip Cohen. Her father was in the catering and food business in the Washington, DC area, where Cass grew up and went to school. Never wanting to be anything other than a singer and performer, Cass honed her talents in summer stock playing the French nurse in *The Boyfriends* before moving to New York, where she soon gained notice. In 1962 she competed, unsuccessfully, against Barbra Streisand for a part in *I Can Get It For You Wholesale*.

In 1963 she formed the folk group The Triumvirate along with Tim Rose and Jim Hendricks, later renamed The Big Three. She also married Hendricks to help him escape the military draft. The band made numerous television appearances on network shows, including *The Danny Kaye Show*. Two albums were recorded before the group added Denny Doherty and called themselves Cass Elliot and The Big Three. Zal Yanovsky took Tim Rose's part when Rose left the group. They renamed the band The Mugwumps and recorded nine songs before they broke up in 1965. Zal went on to form The Lovin' Spoonful with John Sebastian, Denny moved on to The New Journeymen, and Cass went solo, until Denny recommended her to John and Michelle.

Michelle vividly remembers first meeting Cass. "There was a knock on the door. I answered it and, as I opened the door, it hit me all at once. There was Cass Elliot, standing with a big flip and her eyelashes. She had big, fake, eyelashes on. She had a pink angora sweater on and a white pleated skirt.

"'Hi! I'm Cass Elliot.'

"I figured she was.

"'Well, we just took some LSD 25. Want to try some?'

"'Yeah sure.'

"So we gave her the other sugar cube and off we went. It was really an interesting night because Cass and I became very, very, good friends that night. She was a great storyteller, and you never knew if she was telling a huge lie or if it was based on fact — it didn't matter because you loved listening to her. She really knew how to weave a tale."

John had known Cass years earlier when she went by her real name — Naomi Ellen Cohen. "Cass and I grew up in the same town, in Alexandria, Virginia. I had met her because her father had owned a deli. I didn't know it. She reminded me later that I was one of the people she knew about from our town.

"I've always liked the sound of men and women singing together. That's been very important to me. I don't know where it came from — church, people singing together, men and women in a choir. That kind of thing. It's always been the most beautiful thing I've ever heard and it's very integral to my life. I never wanted a group with just all guys or all women. I wanted to mix it together. So, that's what I got."

Like Denny, Cass loved The Beatles, as he recalls. "Cass loved The Beatles — they were English. She started ramming John with The Beatles — the sound, the harmonies, those counterpoints. He started to listen and saw the merit in the arrangements, the vocal arrangements. John has this capacity with numbers, mathematics, which music is. If you can fit the numbers together right, it makes a great sum. With the people he had to work with vocally that was easy for him to do. It wasn't that far from those kind of counterpoint melodies that The Beatles got into. But that was in the songwriting, so he got into the songwriting because of the sound of the arrangements that they had."

Cass had many friends in the music scene. One was Elaine "Spanky" McFarlane, lead singer for the 1960s group Spanky and Our Gang, who became a member of The New Mamas and The Papas in the 1980s. Like Denny, Spanky and Cass were drinking buddies. "Friend-to-friend, she was one of the funniest people I have ever known — just naturally funny," Spanky recalls. "I mean, everything was a big joke to her. We were drinking buddies. We would go to this little bar on Well Street, in the old town, in Chicago, and get drunk every night. We'd make promises about how we were going to be friends for life. If either of us ever made it in the business, we were going to come back and make an album with the other one. We were going to help each other along.

"It's funny because never did I dream I would ever be in The Mamas and The Papas. Whoever thought she would die so young, so tragically, and that I would some day, six, seven years later, take her place. No fortune teller could have predicted it.

"Cass was a great lady. I think everyone who knew her was touched by her sense of humor, her generosity, just the way she was. She was a great singer, too. She had a style — she had her own style. I don't like to say it was Jewish . . . but . . . it was kind of Liza Minnelli. She was, a great, great, singer."

The '60s were half over and The Mamas and The Papas were not a musical entity yet, even though John knew that Michelle, Cass, and Denny were all he needed to work his magic. After one more great escapade "Down in Kokomo," camping on the beach in the Virgin Islands and playing at Duffy's bar in Creeque Alley, "California Dreamin'" would become a reality for The Mamas and The Papas.

Early in 1965, the nucleus of The Mamas and The Papas, less Cass who followed later, embarked upon an Caribbean odyssey that none will forget, especially Denny. "We'd been taking 'controlled substances'. One night we said, 'Let's get out of New York. Let's go somewhere on a vacation, let's do something wild and crazy.' We'd been working our buns off — let's take a rest. There was a map of the world on the wall. We spun Michelle around, blindfolded, and said wherever she puts her finger, we're taking the cash, and the credit card, and we are going there — just go, do wild and crazy things. (Michelle's finger landed on The Virgin Islands.) We went there, spent ten days, to check everything out, came back and collected everybody — Michelle's sister and her boyfriend, our guitar player and his girlfriend, and the dog. Laura (MacKenzie) said she wanted to come with us. 'If you're going, I'm going.' So we took her.

"We had tents, cots, stoves, two motorcycles and an upright bass fiddle. I had a trombone. We went from the airport, all around the island to a place called Redhook, and got a ferry over to St. John. I think John liked the name of the island, St. John — it had a ring. It was a United States National Park. For a nominal fee, you could get a place to put up your tent. I think it was like sixteen bucks a month or something — ridiculous. There was nothing else. It was this little island, in the Caribbean, with peacocks screaming and mongoose running around. There were no snakes — that was nice."

Michelle's version differs slightly from Denny's account. Things took on an added hue when Cass hove into view. "The decision to go to St. Thomas was related to the LSD experience — or we thought it was. Denny, John, and I went first. We were going for a four-day vacation and we ended up staying ten days. We couldn't bring ourselves to think that this was the end of it, so we decided, let's go back to New York, finish off the two dates that we have, and then come back and stay for as long as we want to stay. This seemed very much in keeping with the new experience.

"So, we bought little Honda motorcycles, went to the Army-Navy surplus store, and bought tents and cots and off we went. We took MacKenzie and my dog. We invited my sister, Rusty, and her boyfriend Peter Palafian. We also invited Eric Hoard, a guitar and banjo player, and his girlfriend Nadine. It was great!

"None of us had ever done anything like that before — just forget about New York, forget about everything, let's go live in the islands for a while. We extended an invitation to Cass, but she thought we were all kind of mad.

"She said, 'I know where you are and if I can I'll get down there.'

"We had all these tents set up on the beach in St. John. We had our American Express card and that's what we basically lived on. We bought groceries in St. John. We were having a great time. We did nothing but sing on the beach, swim, and just in general play around and live in the sun. We smoked a lot of pot and took the odd bit of LSD. We were having a great time. We weren't working and we weren't doing anything.

"One day I remember Denny just looking down the beach saying, 'What the hell!' And there came Cass with her shoes in her hands. She said that her wallet had been stolen so she was penniless, but she did have a vial of liquid LSD. That took us through another couple of months."

MacKenzie Phillips has yet another set of memories of this escapade. "I remember all kinds of things. I was about five years old and they were all crazed, living in tents on the beach in the Virgin Islands.

I had my own little pup tent and it was just very strange. They were all on acid, or something. As I said I was just a five-year-old and used to sneak over to the other campsite and steal cereal and food and sneak back.

"There were tons of sailors around. I'd go and smack their butts on the bar stools and get them to buy breakfast. One day, I got this guy to buy me breakfast and then he bought me a pair of shoes. Then I got another guy to buy me breakfast.

"I went back and Dad said, 'Let's go to breakfast.' We go to the same place and the lady says, "Did you know that this is her third breakfast. She's had three sailors in here.' It was wild."

Denny would be the first to admit that the thought of sun-filled days on sandy beaches with inviting warm water and having nothing to do but party, smoke pot, and do LSD had its attractions. But it, too, can pale after a while, especially when boredom sets in, no matter how idyllic the setting. "There was nothing going on. There was this quiet little island with the swamp behind and we were all going slowly crazy. We finally named it Camp Torture. We have to get out of here!

"John was always one to sit and think. 'No, no,' he said, 'this is nice.' But, we're not going anywhere here. The money is going to run out and we're going to have to leave.

"So, John left everyone on the island, took the ferry, put on his Journeyman suit — his three piece suit, the tie and everything. He looked very Madison Avenue and went over to St. Thomas to meet Hugh Duffy, who owned Duffy's of St. Thomas — a hotel. He and John were fast friends. John has a way of charming the apples off the tree. Duffy was starved for something from the mainland.

"'I have all these people, they're over on St. John. They're just sitting in tents. We're a musical group.'

"'A musical group! Music! People from the mainland — come on over to my hotel.'

"Well, about six months later Duffy's hotel no longer existed. We had gutted the inside of the hotel and turned it into a night club. Peter Palafian, who was our road manager later on, had this mad scientist type brain. He went out and scoured the island. He found a lot of electrical instruments and a set of drums. We re-did Duffy's.

"Cass showed up at that point. She didn't come with us initially on any of these trips to the Virgin Islands. She went to DC and started a jazz trio, then wound up back in New York because that didn't make it. She wanted to follow us around. She came down to the island and was waiting on tables. She got there a little late for rehearsal, so she wasn't in the group. She and John had been butting heads for a long time. They were both these very strong personalities.

"We were ripping Duffy's apart inside. We were just gutting the building and throwing it all out in the alleyway. The truck comes and takes it all away. One of the things we were gutting was the ice machine that was out from the bar — we needed the space.

"Cass had now joined us. She was going to do anything she could to stay around. She was coming down Creeque Alley into Duffy's one day and some local workman was ripping the guts out of the ice machine. He took a big coil of copper tubing out of it and threw it out of a window, thinking it was going to land in the pile of garbage. Cass was underneath and it hit her on the top of the head — knocked her cold in Creeque Alley where she was lying in a pile of stuff. We dragged her back upstairs, set her down, and she came to.

"Later on that week she started singing. Before the accident, there was a note she couldn't reach singing with Michelle who's got a soprano voice. Cass didn't have a soprano voice, she had high notes, but not the same timbre as Michelle had. She came up with another note after being hit on the head with this pipe. She could sing all of a sudden. She joined the group at this point."

Cass was very sensitive about her weight, especially when she and Michelle were together. She found a way to sing with the group at Duffy's without having to stand on stage beside Michelle. "While John, Denny and I were singing at Duffy's, Cass was singing at Duffy's, too," Michelle recalls. "But she wouldn't sing on stage because she said that she would never let the audience make a physical distinction between us. We couldn't convince her to sing on stage, but she would sing the fourth part from the back of the room while she was waiting on tables — it worked quite well for a while.

"We were driving Duffy crazy because we were occupying all the rooms in the guest house and he didn't have that income. We weren't exactly drawing in huge crowds of people and he had put a lot of money into us — he built a stage, he bought equipment."

Building codes and fire regulations were the last thing John or Denny thought about when they renovated Duffy's. As Denny later recognized, this error in planning led to their quick exit from the Virgin Islands. "The fire department came and said, 'Duffy, are you people crazy? This is burlap, it's not fireproof.' They closed the place down and we had to redo it," recalls Denny.

"While we were redecorating Duffy's, the Governor's nephew was helping us. He got into the drug bag, at some point, and went home. He was sitting in the middle of his bed screaming, 'They did it! The people at Duffy's did it. Is my head coming off yet? My ears are going. My hair is turning blue.'

"The Governor let us know that he wanted us out of the country with one of those 'don't let the sun go down on you in my county' expressions. We had to get off the island."

A bit of fast talking and some incredibly good luck got them from the Virgin Islands to San Juan, Puerto Rico, where Michelle learned that a rubber check only bounces so far. "We packed our bags and went to the airport — we were really quite broke. We talked Virgin Island's airline into taking this rubber check, but we couldn't talk TWA into doing it once we got to Puerto Rico."

Everyone involved can look back on the experience of trying to get back to New York with twinkling good humor, especially Denny. But at the time, the nine people and a dog didn't find it humorous, especially when they boarded a DC3 for the short hop from St. Thomas to San Juan. "Getting off the island was a rare treat. It was a DC3 where you walked up to your seat. The dog was put in the cargo hold and she yelled and screamed — she was pregnant.

"Nadine was pregnant, Rusty was pregnant, everyone was pregnant, the trees were pregnant. I wasn't pregnant. We got to Puerto Rico, nine people looking like a lost gypsy tribe — we were a very forlorn looking bunch. We had spent all the money. All we had left was the American Express card.

"We went down to the American Express office in San Juan to get another five hundred and gave them the card. They took the card. 'Oh! This is the card.' They took scissors and cut the card in half.

"'What now, John? What are we going to do now?'

"'Don't worry, we'll do something.'

"He went over and talked to one of the desk people. He's mumbling at the desk guy and gives him a piece of paper — it's a check.

"'Are you crazy? Get out of here with that!'

"John tells him that we have nine people, including the kid, and we've got to get back to New York.

"'How are we going to do it?'

"'Beats me.'

"You could see the wheels turning. John asks us how much money we've got. I don't know how much we had, but it was not enough to get nine people and all our bags back to New York. It was going to cost thousands and thousands of dollars.

"'Let's get dressed. Michelle take your red dress, go into the rest room, and put it on. Denny, come on, let's get our Journeymen suits on.'

"We grab a cab and go over to the Hilton. It has a gambling casino in the basement. We walk into the casino and head for the crap table. Michelle picks up the dice, rolls eighteen straight passes — John is betting the money. There's some guy screaming 'Yeah!' We won enough to go back to the airport and buy tickets for nine people and all our bags. The guy at the counter was amazed — we'd only been gone for a couple of hours. John tells him we sold everything — our motorcycles and camping gear. We got on the plane and flew back to New York.

"Things like that have happened to John all his life."

Things were no less hilarious when they arrived back in New York, as Denny continues. "When we left New York, John and Michelle had an apartment on East 7th Street. He gave it to Scott and his girlfriend, who were going to sub-let it until we got back, whenever that might be.

"'Who knows if we'll ever see you again Scott but take care of the apartment until we get home.' Well, apparently Scott and his girlfriend were having a little falling out. The cab pulls up in front of John and Michelle's old apartment, and John gets out after being on this odyssey for months and months in the islands — the planes, the gambling, the pregnant dog. Here comes Scott, down the steps, with his suitcase. He's leaving. They're splitting up.

"'Okay Scott. Thank you very much, I'm going to go to bed.'

"John walks upstairs, right back into his apartment like nothing happened. Bingo! the door closes and he's home. He had just spent a year on the road."

In the song *Creeque Alley*, John and Michelle put a fine cap on that year in the Virgin Islands, forever evoked by the final verse. They also projected the course of the subsequent career of The Mamas and The Papas:

> *Broke — busted — disgusted, agents can't be trusted*
> *and Michie wants to go to the sea.*
> *Cass can't make it, she says we'll have to fake it,*
> *we knew she would come eventually.*
> *Greasin' on American Express card; tent's low rent,*
> *but keepin' out the heat's hard.*
> *Duffy's good vibrations*
> *and our imaginations can't go on indefinitely;*
> *And California dreamin' is becomin' a reality . . .*

The Mamas and The Papas celebrate signing their first recording contract with Dunhill in September 1965. (Photo MCA Archives)

THE MAMAS & THE PAPAS

YOUNG GIRLS ARE COMING TO THE CANYON

Twelve Thirty (Young Girls Are Coming To The Canyon)

I used to live in New York City
Everything there was dark and dirty
Outside my window was a steeple
With a clock that always said twelve thirty

Young girls are coming to the canyon
And in the morning I can see them walkin'
I can no longer keep my blinds drawn
And I can't keep myself from talkin'

At first so strange to feel so friendly
To say 'Good mornin'' and really mean it
To feel these changes happenin' in me
But not to notice till I feel it . . .

(John Phillips, ASCAP)

When John and Michelle Phillips arrived back in New York from the Virgin Islands, they thought they were penniless, but thanks to an unexpected royalty check they had enough cash to embark on another adventure. John decided that they would take Horace Greeley's advice and 'Go West'. As John tells the tale, "I went to the bank and found there was about $1,200 that had come from a royalty check — from somewhere that we had no idea about. I closed out the account and drew the money out. We split the money up evenly between us all. Michelle's and my share was like $400 bucks. Denny got $400, Cass got $400. We decided to go West.

"We went to one of those 'you drive our car to another coast' places. We put on our best clothes and Michelle did her hair in a honeycomb. I had a preacher's suit on. We walked in and talked to this nice old lady. We completely conned her. She said that we were the best looking couple she had ever seen who wanted to drive a car from New York to California. Little did she know we had these acid freaks waiting to go West.

"She said, 'You'll have to leave us a twenty-five dollar deposit, then we'll give you the keys to the car.'

"We had all our credentials — which were mostly phoney. We went back to 7th and O and we took a sort of street collection to get the twenty-five dollars. Every friend in New York, we'd call up, we'd get like a dollar-fifty here, seventy-five cents there. We finally get the twenty-five dollars and a tank of gas, plus our four hundred bucks to travel and eat on. We were ready to go across the country — we got it all together.

"It was a Cadillac limousine, a brand new Cadillac limousine — the woman trusted us that much. That's where she went wrong. She probably lost her whole business after doing this, I am sure. We start taking meths and driving across the country. We would take turns driving night-and-day, then we'd stop some place, for a couple of days, so we'd get there on time. We would drive twenty-four straight hours and sleep thirty-six and lose twelve hours in the process or else go mountain climbing in the Grand Canyon. Wow! See the colors.

"We be-decked the car with flowers — this was before 'Wear Flowers in Your Hair,' the San Francisco song. We'd pull into these little towns, like Fort Collins, Colorado, and they would see this Cadillac limousine coming down the street with a huge bouquet. We'd be driving down the street and these guys with cowboy hats and six guns on were spitting out tobacco. It was a strange, interesting, sight.

"I wrote a lot of songs on the trip. I wrote *Straight Shooter* and *Go Where You Wanna Go*. I write very well when I am driving for some reason. I write about my life, my friends, my lovers — things that I observe. If it takes more than twenty minutes, it's no good. If I can't write it in twenty minutes, then it's over. It's like being in an oven too long. It's tough. It has to be like just bing! All the songs I've ever written that have been popular songs have only taken me minutes to write. I can do it anywhere. I've written songs in a room full of people, by myself, on walks, in cars. I like cars. It's fun to be jumbling along the freeway or somewhere and suddenly I pull over and write. I've written quite a few songs that way.

"It sounds corny but I have a sensitivity — caring for other people. I want everyone to have food, shelter, and clothing. My songs are not for the most part boy-meets-girl songs. They're like *California Dreamin'* or *Go Where You Wanna Go*. What I really care about most is conceptualism. I'm always finding scraps of paper and notebooks that I've lost. There's a song called *She Gotch She*. I wrote the whole thing in one night. I made myself write all the lyrics out — five verses. Then, I lost it. Later, we were doing a new album and I looked through all my cases, all my bags, and I found this tape that I had done at this place called Phantom Studios, in New York — just myself and a guitar. There it was, every word was on the track. We recorded it again the next day before we lost it. I couldn't believe it.

"But that happens all the time. I find songs that I didn't write very quickly. If I can't just sit down and write the song, it's always corny, always belabored, too flowery. The songs that you can sit down and just rip off, in twenty minutes, are the ones that really last and become standards."

Denny had it all worked out right down to how many travel days and how many free car days before they had to return the Cadillac. "It was one of those deals — you pay for the gas, they reimburse you. If you've got a couple of hundred dollars you can do it — we did! We had six or seven days to get it there, so we figured if we got it there in three we'd have the car four days to drive around — which we did.

We slept in the car, lived in the car. We killed the car, somewhere near Denver. The car really didn't make it over those mountains too swift.

"We stopped in Vegas and got dressed up in the clothes again to make another score at the casinos. It didn't happen in Vegas the way it happened in San Juan, though. Coming over the San Bernadino foothills Michelle wanted to drive because she knows the freeway system. I'm curled up in the back seat, in the fetal position, so I don't see that much of it. We're on the Harbor Freeway. I'm seeing smoke. What's going on? There's a lot of burning. People are off on the side of the freeway. Turn the radio on. There are snipers on the Harbor Freeway. We're on the Harbor Freeway! Cars pile up, there are snipers — it was the Watt's riots.

"We immediately got off the Harbor Freeway. There was a guy, in a Jeep, with a 50 caliber machine gun going, 'Turn around!'

"I'm saying, 'Backup Michelle. Just move it!'

"We went to stay with Michelle's friend, Marga. We stayed there for two weeks watching the riots on television. Welcome to Los Angeles."

Los Angeles was a new world for John and Denny, though for Michelle the city was home, and Cass was already a resident, having moved there with Jim Hendricks when she returned from the Virgin Islands. "One thing I remember very well when we got to L.A. — I had never really been down Sunset Boulevard," recalls John. "I don't think Denny had ever been out to the West Coast. Michelle had — she was just thrilled out of her mind. We drove Sunset, in this Cadillac limousine, which fitted right in, perfectly. In L.A. it was great! This convertible, full of girls, pulled up next to us and Denny put the window down.

"'What group are you with?'

"'Farmer's Mutual.'

"We went on.

"Cass had married this guy named Jimmy Hendricks (not to be confused with Jimi Hendrix) to keep him out of the draft. It was during Vietnam days. This is the summer of '65. All of us were living in their apartment. We had a couple of cats and the girls would beg for money for cat food on Sunset Strip. The money actually went to the cat food. Denny and I were taking steaks out of supermarkets — wearing big coats. We were taking a lot of drugs at the time. It seemed like the thing to do. We were expanding our minds. We had no idea it was Russian roulette, at the time."

For Denny, arriving in Los Angeles, with no place to stay, and finding out Cass and Jimmy had an apartment seemed like a godsend — until they saw the apartment. "The lights were turned off, the gas was turned off, and there was a Marshall's notice of eviction on the door. We were not there for a long time but for a good time, and there was nothing to cook on. In California bathrooms, they don't have any central heating, as such, they have an element that heats up. Being from Halifax and having to make do with what you have on the road, the wheels began to turn. If I take this out of the wall and turn it this way, I'll have a hot plate and it will work. That was the stove. We were living on franks and beans, on top of the toilet, in the bathroom.

"In the meantime, we were seeing record companies and drove up to San Francisco to see Frank Weber in a '65 Ford LTD we purchased on Scott McKenzie's credit card. John said he wouldn't pass the card. Like a twit, I said that I would and signed Scott's name.

"We drive back to L.A. and stay at the Landmark Hotel. The car is stolen and driven to Mexico. It's stripped — everything! Scott never heard about that until years later. He kept getting these bills from his credit card."

Many of their hijinks came to an end when Barry McGuire, who had just released his hit single *Eve Of Destruction*, introduced the members of The Mamas and The Papas to his producer, Lou Adler of Dunhill Records. Over the next three years, The Mamas and The Papas would record a string of hits, starting with *California Dreamin'* in November 1965, that would define the 'California' sound and lifestyle for an entire generation of Americans.

For the Mamas and the Papas, 1965 and 1966 were truly remarkable years. Not only did the band secure a recording contract with Dunhill, they released five singles that charted in the Top Five — *Go Where You Wanna Go*, *California Dreamin'*, *Monday, Monday*, *I Saw Her Again*, and *Words Of Love*. *Monday, Monday* hit Number 1 on 7 May 1996. They also released two albums — IF YOU CAN BELIEVE YOUR EYES AND EARS, which became a Number 1 album on 21 May 1966, and the self-titled THE MAMAS AND THE PAPAS. In less than a year, The Mamas and The Papas became America's answer to The Beatles, creating the so-called "California sound" that scores of other bands would imitate with relative degrees of success, fostering the so-called flower power movement on the West Coast, and playing a central role in the Monterey Pop Festival during the "summer of love" in 1967. These halcyon years were not without turbulence, however, as Michelle would be 'fired' from the band in mid-1966.

In a strange moment of clairvoyance or bravado, John Phillips predicted — indeed promised — such success, as he recalls. "We were driving around the night The Beatles played the Hollywood Bowl for the first time. You can go behind the Hollywood Bowl, way up in the hills, and overlook. You can't really see the act, but you can see the audience and the sound reflects beautifully.

"Cass was saying, 'God, wouldn't it be great if someday we could actually get to play the Hollywood Bowl and do all those things?'

"We all loved The Beatles and their music and everything. So, with the brashness that I had, I said, 'Well, I'll tell you something. Next year, this time not only will we play the Hollywood Bowl, we'll have a Number 1 record, a Number 1 album, and we'll win a Grammy Award — I promise you this.'

"I don't know how I got the power to promise these things — it's beyond me. I think it was a little help from acid at the time. All those things came true. We were able to play the Hollywood Bowl, twice in that year, and we did have a Number 1 single and album that year."

Their string of good luck began when Barry McGuire, formerly of the New Christy Minstrels, who had just recorded his huge hit *Eve Of Destruction* with Dunhill, dropped by Cass's apartment where Denny, John, and Michelle were also living at the time.

"Barry McGuire was already a good friend from the Village and from the New Christy Minstrels," as John tells the story. "He had always been on the folk music scene. We'd known him for years. Barry had *The Eve of Destruction* record. He used to come by on his Triumph 750 motorcycle and turn us green with envy. The first time he came by, Denny was taking the heater out of the bathroom and making a hot plate out of it. It's a funny thing about L.A.

They have these gas fireplaces and no one needs a fire — very strange.

"He heard us rehearsing and said, 'I think you should come down and meet this guy Lou Adler who is a record producer. He's very good. I think he'll like the stuff you're doing.' Barry told Lou that he wanted him to hear us sing because we were really good. Lou said he didn't know. He was very aloof, at first. We waited at the studio about two hours while we did these tracks. The tracks weren't particularly appealing, I didn't think anyway.

"'What am I supposed to do with these guys, Barry,' said Lou.

"'I want you to hear them sing, they are really great.'

"We were in studio 'C'. We started singing. Lou came in. Our backs were turned, we didn't even see him. We were singing with the twelve-string guitar, which is all we ever had to rehearse with. We had all the vocal parts. They were crisp and clean and neat. Overtones rang through the room. We had the whole first album already written and arranged. All it needed was drums, bass, and piano — it was all there.

"Lou almost died. He turned purple. He couldn't believe his eyes or his ears. He made up the title for our first album that night — IF YOU CAN BELIEVE YOUR EYES AND YOUR EARS.

"'What do you need?'

"'Well,' I said, 'we need everything. We're penniless. We have no food. We have no car. We have no house, no clothing — nothing at all.

"'Come back to the office at nine o'clock in the morning. Don't be late, whatever you do,'

"In the meantime, Nick Venet had come by. He was a record producer. He had heard us sing. He told us he had sold his car, some kind of sports car, this morning for ten thousand dollars and he'd give us the ten thousand immediately if we would sign with him and not go and see Lou. But we gave our word to Lou, and we had this strange kind of acid mentality, you know — you have to be true to what you say and this whole thing.

"We were trying to wake each other up because we had stayed up all night drinking. We showed up around noon. We got to his office and he is trying to play it cool, but you could see his hand tapping. Lou gave us five thousand dollars. We liked Lou a lot. He was a very talented man — still is a very talented man."

Denny's version of what happened when Lou Adler offered them the contract throws new shading on John's bravado. "John, being John, steps right up," Denny recounts.

"'Oh! What do we want? What we want Lou, really, is a steady flow of money from your office to our house, but we don't have a house yet. If we had a house we couldn't get there from here because we have no car — Money! House! Car!'

"'Right away,' Lou says, 'don't worry.' He gave us five thousand dollars.

"We went out and found a house in the paper. Lou had a friend in east L.A., who had a car lot, and we wound up with a '59 Buick convertible that we called Harold the Bleek. That all happened in two or three days. Two or three days later John and I are driving along the L.A. freeway system and we're in this Buick convertible going, 'Not too shabby, what do you think? Not too bad.' We hadn't recorded a note yet."

Lou Adler and Dunhill Records played a central role in the history of The Mamas and The Papas. Dunhill founder Pierre Cossette tells the story of his label. "We started off from dead scratch. Lou Adler was working at Columbia and we brought Lou in as producer. He found a kid named Johnny Rivers. We recorded Johnny at the Whisky A Go Go, and we put Ann Margaret, a student at North Western, in the Go Go cage. She wanted to get into show business. Johnny did great. He came out with a number one single and a number one album. Then, we really got lucky with a guy named Barry McGuire on *The Eve Of Destruction*. Our second record was a number one single. Barry kept telling us about this group that had formed called The Mamas and The Papas. So, in come The Mamas and The Papas. We signed them.

"I remember in those days we shared office space with lawyers and dentists, so the musicians had no place to rehearse. We put them in an office. It was very crowded in there and we got a lot of complaints, so they would have to come back after the offices were closed.

"We had a guy named Jerry Moss who was promoting our records for fifty bucks a week. He had this guy Dore Alpert who wanted to do a bullfighter-instrumental sort of a thing. I turned that down because, in those days, I was the sole investor in this company and I just didn't feel that an instrumental record could happen — it happened. Dore Alpert changed his name around to Herb Alpert and recorded *Lonely Bull*. Herb and Jerry Moss raised a few bucks here and there, like a garage band does, and they made this bullfight record. That was the beginning of A&M Records."

The first job that The Mamas and The Papas had with Dunhill was singing back-up vocals for Barry McGuire's album, HANG ON SLOOPY, as John explains, which was to include Barry singing *California Dreamin'*. "The first project we worked on was singing background on the Barry McGuire album that Lou Adler was recording at the time. Lou asked me to let Barry record *California Dreamin'* and for us to sing background. I played guitar on it and we all sang background. It was sort of our theme song. Barry sang the exact same track that *California Dreamin'* is on now, but an octave lower — Barry's voice is an octave lower than Denny's.

"Lou came to me and said, 'Do you think you could go to Barry and say you don't want him to record your song, it doesn't sound right. We could put Denny up an octave higher, against the background track that's already finished.

"'Sure. I don't think Barry will say anything.'

"I went to Barry and talked to him about it. He didn't care one way or the other. He'd take his clothes off and jump in the pool. He was happy.

"'Yeah! Go ahead. It's your song, it's not mine. Do what you want with it.'

"So, we went in and recorded it. Denny did a spectacular vocal on it and then the vocal arrangement came out beautifully. That's how *California Dreamin'* came about. It was really meant for Barry McGuire.

"On Barry's first album, HANG ON SLOOPY, we sing all the backgrounds. It's sort of a collector's item. You hear The Mamas and The Papas' background harmonies all the way through the whole thing."

The story behind their only Number 1 hit is no less intriguing, as John tells the tale of the genesis of *Monday, Monday*. "I guess the most popular song with The Mamas and The Papas was *Monday, Monday*. It was one of the very few songs that I've ever written that was not about a personal situation or about a friend or concept. I decided to write a hit song. I'd never done that before and I haven't done it since. Denny was yelling at me about writing songs.

"'Why don't you write some more songs — we need some more songs.'

"Okay, let's sit down . . . I'm going to write a song tonight about a universal subject. Something that everyone understands — so I'll write a song about Monday — so I wrote *Monday, Monday*. Since then I have had people come up to me with about thirty different interpretations of what *Monday, Monday* really means.

"'That was a girl, wasn't it?'

"'Sure it was a girl.'

"'You don't like the day of the week, right?'

"'That's right, you got it.'

"I have no idea what the song means. I can't make any sense of the lyric. But it was about a sort of universal theme, like Thank God It's Friday. If you wrote a song called 'Thank God It's Friday' you'd probably have a Top Forty single."

Bah-da bah-da-da-da
Bah-da bah-da-da-da
Bah-da-bah-da-da-da

Monday, Monday, so good to me
Monday mornin', it was all I hoped it would be
On Monday mornin', Monday mornin' couldn't guarantee
That Monday evenin' you would still be here with me

Monday, Monday, can't trust that day
Monday, Monday, sometimes it just turns out that way
Oh Monday mornin', you gave me no warnin' of what was to be
Oh Monday, Monday, how could you leave and not take me . . .

Michelle and Cass found no promise in *Monday, Monday* when they first heard John sing the song, but Lou Adler liked it and insisted it be the follow-up single to *California Dreamin'*. "I hated it!" Michelle declares. "I remember when John first started playing the song for us. Cass and I heard the song and I said, 'God John, I hate to be so negative, but this song is really pretentious.'

"'What are you talking about? This is a great song.' He said that he wanted to write a song with international appeal.

"'Well that's great John, but this is a very contrived song.'

"He played it for Lou. Lou loved it. We recorded the song and Lou told us that it was going to be our next single after *California Dreamin'*. I was struck dumb!

"'How could you do this to us? This is going to be the end of what was a very promising career for us.'

"'Michelle, you girls do the singing and I'll do the releasing — okay?'

"I thought, 'Well, fine, but you know it's going nowhere.'

"It shot to the top of the charts faster than any record we ever had. To this day, it is the biggest record that The Mamas and The Papas ever had. I like it now, I like it a lot — a girl has the right to change her mind."

Although Denny instigated the writing of *Monday, Monday*, he also didn't like the song. "*Monday, Monday* — I didn't want to record it. I didn't like the song. What's the song mean? It's a song about a day of the week. We were spending hours on this song, and who knew, who knew? This turns out to be a Number 1 record. Well, I guess, well stupid me — what do I know?"

It took David Crosby of The Byrds to convince Denny that *Monday, Monday* was a bona fide hit. "I think nineteen weeks had gone by since the recording session. David Crosby comes and says, 'Hey! Congratulations man.'

"I'm going, 'What? David, what is it?'

"'You have a hit record.'

"'What are you talking about?'

He was carrying *Billboard*. 'You're on the charts.'

'No kidding? What does that mean?'

'You've got a hit record man.'

"It was the biggest record in Boston in twenty years. Is that good?

"The rest is history."

Much of the success of these songs can be attributed to John Phillips' dedication to perfection in the studio. "Starting from the beginning, from the tracks,' John explains, "it has to be done properly all the way through all the steps. In those days, we didn't have thirty-two track machines — we had four track machines so you would constantly have to do what they call 'bouncing'. You would sing live to track and take the track that was on the machine and put both of them onto another track on the same machine, always leaving two tracks open. Once you were committed to it, you couldn't bring it back. So we had to be very careful.

"Fortunately we had a real genius in the booth named Bones Howe who was an incredible engineer. We had Larry Knechtel playing piano, Hal Blaine on drums, and Joe Osborn on bass. I was playing twelve-string. That was our basic unit that we recorded with. It was very tight. It worked out so good that we had everything nice and crisp the whole time.

"But as far as the freedom goes, we would work in the studio sometimes to a counter effect, actually. We worked too long. I remember Cass fainting, quite a few times, in the studio from over exertion. We'd been there sixteen hours trying to do the eighteenth or nineteenth take to get the sound that we wanted — it was just too much for the human body to withstand."

Denny is sure that it was the infamous "fifth" voice that kept everyone partially sane and pressing on. "The first sessions were marathons. We'd rehearse a lot at home, but getting into the studio, things would change. When a problem would pop up, John would attack the problem — that might take ten hours for that one thing. We'd finish that problem and then we'd go home, come back and start again — they were marathon sessions. They would go on, and on, and on.

"Lou Adler's head would be hitting the console. 'It's a wrap. Go to sleep!' There were big parties that they'd try to keep under control, as much as possible. We'd get those in the studio to make it sound like a rehearsal.

"There was a 'fifth' voice. We can rehearse for another ninety-eight hours. When we were singing really well, overtones we used to call it, 'Harvey' would show up. This phantom overtone voice, up on top above everything else. It wasn't really there. We'd be singing, really close together, with our heads together trying to work on a part and we'd hear him — Harvey's here! Okay, we can do it now. We found him. When Harvey would appear, the arrangement usually would gel."

John also speaks of a similar haunting while arranging the songs. "Arranging is more of an exercise in musical skills. I don't read a word of music at all. I read no music. So everything that I do, I do by ear. Back in the '60s when we'd have big string sections, like thirty or forty players, I'd have to hum the parts that I wanted them to play and they would write them down.

"They'd say, 'This will never work.'

"'Give it a try, give it a try.'

"I've always had an ability to hear three kinds of parts in my head at the same time as I arrange. It's really what The Mamas and The Papas had been built on. I had always liked the sound of men and women singing together. I tried to keep it very simple and moving rather than intricate. I guess the most intricate things are the simplest when you get down to it.

"Everything happens by accident. I'll wake up, in the middle of the night, or I'll have a dream, especially when I'm recording. I dream a lot of the arrangements. It's like a haunting. It's like a twenty-four hour a day job. I go to sleep but I don't really go to sleep. I go back to the studio.

"I guess writing is what brings the most satisfaction to me and it's the hardest to do. It's the hardest to conceive the work and actually put it on paper. I've actually gone through a dream sequence where I've written a song, awakened, and been able to write the words down, get the guitar and have the song finished. I've also written during functional blackouts.

"One song, Me And My Uncle, has been recorded by The Grateful Dead, Judy Collins, Glen Campbell, and a bunch of people. I have no recollection of writing it whatsoever. They keep sending me checks and I keep accepting them, so it worked out pretty well, but I don't remember it at all."

"Performing is great because it is instant gratification — but it doesn't last."

Throughout 1966 The Mamas and The Papas did just that — perform and record, record and perform. They seemed to be on television every week — Shindig, Hollywood Palace with Arthur Godfrey, American Bandstand with Dick Clark, Hollywood A Go Go, and the Ed Sullivan Show, where they became almost regulars over the next few years. The band dressed quintessentially "hippie," with Cass taking the lead on stage wearing her suede boots and tent dresses, Denny wearing Nehru jackets and a 'far-out' look, Michelle, the flower-child, and John in the background, looking even taller than he was wearing a fur hat. The Mamas and The Papas quickly became the image of the California hippie movement for the rest of America.

This image was created in part by the infamous cover for their first album, IF YOU CAN BELIEVE YOUR EYES AND EARS, which portrays The Mamas and The Papas posed in a bathtub, Michelle stretched out across John, Cass, and Denny, all fully clothed. Guy Webster, who took this photograph, recalls how John Phillips and Lou Adler intended the cover to be sensational. "I was working with Lou Adler at his newly-formed company, Dunhill Records," Webster explains, "shooting album covers. I had just finished art school and that was the first major album that I produced, the famous cover with the bathtub scene. It sort of represented a new kind of freedom that rock'n'roll suggested. I didn't actually pick that picture — I thought it was almost too far out to be done. But Lou and John and the rest of us altogether liked that picture a lot and figured it would be explosive. And it was. It caused a sensation. The toilet seat had to be covered with a sticker by the company in order for it to get on to the racks. You'll find some covers — they're kind of collector's pieces now — before the sticker was put on the toilet. So, it's kind of like a Beatles mystique.

"The fun thing about that shooting was that I had never been truly high before. I had a few joints once in a while, but never anything like that day. I got high with the group, so that sort of came out of that freedom that marijuana might give you, and we started experimenting, clowning around, laughing, and we ended up in the bathroom. I didn't even realize I was high until afterwards, until after I came down. I said, geez, what the hell did we shoot here. I had a great time and I loved working with them — that kind of freedom."

As Webster recognized, the band members were highly photogenic. "Cass. Exquisite. Her size, she had great beauty and confidence about her and she was great to photograph. I used to photograph her for fashion things for outside the music business. She could pull anything off. And she was very bright.

"Denny was incredibly good looking. John had a great majesty about him, kind of a new way of dressing that was uniquely his. And of course, Michelle, who couldn't have been more gorgeous and was like working with a fashion model. We did a lot of fashion layouts together subsequently for fashion magazines and local magazines."

Not only was the appearance of The Mamas and The Papas unique on their first album, so was the music, as music historian Pete Fornatale recalls. "IF YOU COULD BELIEVE YOUR EYES AND EARS arrived at my college radio station where I was working at the time. In an era of fresh sounds, it was one of the freshest, both visually and aurally. There was something about the band that was quite wonderful, right from the opening notes of that record.

"It was also at a time when the industry was not strictly relying on singles any more. We had just come out of the Top 40 era and now suddenly albums as a whole were beginning to make an impact. The Mamas and The Papas had it both ways. They had hit singles, the two big ones from that album, *California Dreamin'* and *Monday, Monday*. They also had all those wonderful songs behind the album that backed it up and made it one of the strongest debut releases that I have ever heard by any group."

Fornatale itemizes the qualities that made this album and the band so strong. "The first thing that comes to mind is the sexual integration of the group. I don't think there had been a group of equal partners, men and women, prior to that time. Secondly, John's writing — John's lyric writing. If you look back at it, we had just come through the earth tremors created by the British Invasion, and suddenly America, which had invented rock'n'roll, was put in a position of having to defend its turf. The American response came in the form of mainly folk-rock singers and writers. Bob Dylan certainly spearheaded that. Paul Simon and Art Garfunkel were part of it, John Sebastian, The Lovin' Spoonful, Roger McGuinn, David Crosby and The Byrds. An equal part of this movement was The Mamas and The Papas with John's songs.

"If you look back on the songs of The Mamas and The Papas, they were really precursors of a lot of the social changes that we've gone through in the years since. What are those songs if not about male-female relationships both within the group and on a larger symbolic level in society.

"For the people who made a Mamas and Papas song *their* song, nostalgia is certainly going to be an element of their appreciation today. But I think there is more to that. I think there was more in the creation of those records and in the creation of those sounds that continues to have an impact today. While it might not be felt through the presence of John and the group itself, it is certainly being felt through their heirs — and by that, I mean Fleetwood Mac, The Mamas and The Papas of the '70s. There is no question that Fleetwood Mac built their very large success on the foundations laid by The Mamas and The Papas in the '60s. If you were looking for it in the '80s, you can find it in groups like Vangelis who acknowledge John Phillips and The Mamas and The Papas as a main inspiration."

After the Number 1 success of their first album came their second, THE MAMAS AND THE PAPAS, in August, which included the songs *Trip*, *Stumble and Fall*, *Dancing Bear*, *Dancing In The Street*, *Words Of Love*, and *I Saw Her Again*. Not only were *Words Of Love* and *I Saw Her Again* top five hits, they recorded in lyrics the love affairs which inspired John's songwriting. *I Saw Her Again* was inspired by John's fears that Michelle and Denny were having an affair, another of his prognostications that would come true:

> I saw her again last night
> And you know that I shouldn't
> To string her along's just not right
> If I couldn't I wouldn't
>
> But what can I do, I'm lonely too
> And it makes me feel so good to know
> You'll never leave me . . .
>
> Everytime I see that girl
> You know I want to lay down and die
> But I really need that girl
> Don't know why I'm livin' a lie
> It makes me wanna cry . . .

Ironically, Denny was given co-credit for this song with John.

With the success of their chart-topping records came fame and money — more money than the individual members of The Mamas and The Papas ever imagined, as Michelle recalls. "The money came overnight. One day we were poor, one day we were rich — and that's how it happened. I don't remember any in-between moments. It was from total poverty to having so much money that we didn't know what to do with it. It was like winning a lottery.

"We had an incredible knack for spending it. We could spend money faster than we could make it, which wasn't hard to do. We would go into a Gucci and we'd buy out the store. We only traveled around in our own little Lear jet. We vacationed a lot — we didn't like to work all that much.

"We worked a lot in '66, then Cass got pregnant and we had to lighten up the load for a while until after she had the baby. We liked to go to Hawaii. We liked those kind of dates — spend a week-and-a-half in Hawaii to do a date. I still pretty much feel the same way about working. I love to work, but I'd still prefer to do it where I'm going to have some fun.

"So, the money was coming. We were all making a lot of money and spending it like mad. We just assumed that the money would always be coming in because we really assumed, at that point, that we would always be together.

"We had a lot of internal problems, but we thought that it would go on for a long time."

Like Michelle, Denny knew how to enjoy his new-found wealth. He, too, embarked upon an hedonistic lifestyle. "I don't know where the money came from or went. I knew that when the fridge was full, I was happy. The lights were still on — good, 'cause I was still in the bathroom cooking on a thermidor, in my head.

"Publishing, that's where the money is. John and Michelle were getting, I don't know what, but they moved to Bel Air with the swimming pools, the Rolls Royces, and the Ferraris. I'm up in Laurel Canyon, in a very nice house — fourteen rooms. Cass was over in Nichols Canyon having a good time. Rudy Vallee was her neighbor. I just kept my party going, very nice."

The band, however, would not even survive 1967 intact because of those 'internal problems' Michelle alludes to, including drug abuse and adultery, vices of the 'sex, drugs, and rock'n'roll' 1960s lifestyle The Mamas and The Papas came to epitomize. John and Denny first recognized they were abusing drugs following the recording of their first album, as John recalls. "After we had finished the album, we were still taking LSD by the handful. We had no idea of the danger of LSD. Our porch started rattling at breakfast. Little fuzzy creatures would run by, things like that. Denny and especially I got very thin and very ill. We were eating a lot of rice and ying yang and all that.

"We went to this doctor, who Lou recommended. His name was Dr Cohen. He ran the brand new substance abuse ward at UCLA. We walked in and talked to him for a while.

"'Well, you two boys seem very nervous. I want to show you something.' He took us to this ward of people who had taken LSD and who had never come back from their initial trip — or their thousandth trip. It didn't seem to matter which trip it was because they hadn't come back. It was like going through a snake pit. You couldn't believe the illusions and hallucinations that they were having — and their behavior.

"Dr Cohen said, 'You are probably about two or three trips from this. I think you should stop now. How many times have you guys taken acid?'

"I said, 'Well, I don't know. We take it every day — doesn't everyone?'

"We were really under the impression that all musicians were taking acid every day. We were part of a sub-culture that was just beginning to grow around '65 and '66. It culminated around 1970 after Woodstock. Doing things that were really illegal, but, at the same time, they seem revolutionary and were for the good of the country and for the good of you. It was a real contradictory part to play in the role of society. If you weren't arrested a couple of times a week for civil disobedience, you were just nobody. You had to have lunch in the dean's office, at least once a week, no matter who the dean was."

There had always been a sexual attraction between Michelle and Denny, dating back to their adventure in the Virgin Islands. John had suspected they were having an affair in late 1965 when he wrote

I Saw Her Again. Michelle is quite candid about her relationship with Denny — and conscious that she knew she was potentially hurting not only John, her husband, but also Cass, who cared for Denny. "We had a lot of internal problems in the group," Michelle explains, "the major one being that Denny and I had an affair. When this surfaced, it was terribly painful for John and hard for John to accept that his wife and best friend had an affair. To Cass, it was the greatest betrayal of all. She was very much in love with Denny. She had always hoped that someday she and Denny would actually be together. It was a betrayal of my husband and it was a betrayal of my best friend, Cass. It was very difficult to overcome.

"Once the information came out, we tried to patch it up. Denny and I, obviously, were never going to do that again. Cass and I were going to see it through this crisis. The group was going to continue.

"It wasn't that easy for me and John. We found it harder and harder to live together. John and I decided to live apart. This was before we had moved to Bel Air. John and Denny moved into the Woods Drive house. It had a sunken fireplace pit and pool at a hundred and ten degrees. There were floating gardenias in the pool and every girl in town was up there. They were living the lives of two rock'n'roll bachelors."

For Denny this was also a bitter experience; he also saw Michelle taking advantage of the rock'n'roll lifestyle to the maximum. "Michelle and I had an affair. That sort of got smoothed over, but John and Michelle never really got back together. So she was off. I wasn't going to get involved with that thing any more so I backed off.

"Now, if you and your girlfriend are in a band — or you and your wife are doing anything where you have to be involved in the business of operating that particular business for eight hours-a-day and then you go home — problems can arise. Who are you with when you go home — the same person you were at work with for eight hours and then go to bed to sleep? You can't. You don't go home with her. She goes some place else, then you go home.

"What is she doing? You're climbing up balconies looking in windows and going crazy trying to check it out. Where's your wife?

"John just couldn't handle that. She didn't mind. She was having a great time — the best of both worlds. 'I'm a rock star and I'm free as a bird. My husband, oh, he's just silly.'"

For years, John had conducted a number of affairs, with the knowledge of his first wife, Susie, and Michelle. If John could play the field, Michelle reasoned, so could she. She took up with Gene Clark of The Byrds, an affair that resulted in her being 'fired' from The Mamas and The Papas by John on 4 June 1966 just shortly before the single *I Saw Her Again* was released. "I was quietly having an affair of my own, which I felt entitled to have . . . by the way!" Michelle discloses. "I wasn't with John and it seemed that I certainly was entitled to this affair. Of course, I hadn't really realized the complexities of it. I was having this affair with Gene Clark from The Byrds. John, I think, had heard about it, but as long as we were never seen in public together, and as long as he didn't have people talking about it, he was pretty much okay about it until one night.

"We were doing a concert outside of L.A., and Gene said, 'Well, I've never seen you guys in concert.'

"'No problem, I'll get you tickets.'

"So I called the Dunhill Record office and said, 'Please make sure Gene Clark has two tickets.'

"'No, problem.'

"Since they didn't know about our affair they gave Gene these first row tickets in Theater in the Round. It never crossed my mind that he would be right up front — it never crossed my mind.

"When we came out — Cass and I led — the first thing we saw was Gene Clark sitting in the front row with a big red shirt on. Cass saw it. Cass knew all about it. She grabbed me and we went to that side of the stage so John and Denny wouldn't.

"We started singing and pretty soon Cass and I were having a great time flirting with Gene and, more or less, forgetting about John and Denny. We were right into the middle of a song when John took his mike and yelled into it.

"'Get the fuck over here!'

"Cass and I realized that he had seen this exchange between Gene and ourselves. My heart just sank because he was so angry. Imagine how angry he must have been to have said this so the entire audience could have heard it. Cass and I went to the other side of the stage. The Papas came over to this side of the stage and we finished the concert.

"I ran off the stage.

"John ran after me. 'That's it, you're fired!'

"That was not one of the possibilities that I had thought of — that I could be fired from the group. I mean, after all, I was Mama Michelle. I just didn't think that could ever happen. I went outside to the parking lot. I was still kind of trying to get it. It was my birthday, too. I was going back to Laurel Canyon for my birthday party.

"I remember looking at John and saying, 'You know John, I knew you were really upset, but I don't think you have the legal right to fire me.'

"'Well, we'll just see about that, won't we? Because, you are fired!'

"I had my birthday party. I didn't really think of it too seriously. I thought things would settle down.

"I didn't hear from them for a couple of days, and then the letter arrived on June 28, 1966. It was a very brutal letter. It was signed by John, Cass, and Denny. It said, basically, 'Thanks for your services to date. Your services will no longer be needed. You are now officially out of this group and thank you very much, but don't call yourself Mama Michelle any more because you are no longer in the group.'

"I was completely torn up by the letter. I was certain that things had to work themselves out — they couldn't be serious. It was a moment that was a real awakening for me. I started to see the kind of damage I had done within the group. It was a terribly frightening time for me."

With Michelle fired, the remaining three had a decision to make. It was probably harder on Denny than the other two. "We go out and get a replacement for Michelle or we call it quits.

"John says, 'It's over, it's finished. I can't do it.'

"I can understand. I mean, who couldn't? Well, John could, I'm sure, if he put his mind to it. Later on he did."

Rather than disband, they decided to replace Michelle, choosing Lou Adler's girlfriend, Jill Gibson, a Michelle look-a-like, as the new Mama. "They replaced me with Lou Adler's girlfriend, Jill Gibson," Michelle comments, bitterly. "John, I think, took great pleasure in replacing me with Jill because he said, 'Replacing you is going to be easy.' It was like he just turned around the room and said, 'You will be the new Mama.' It was crushing to me that I was replaceable — and it was easy to do. John was making a point. He knew exactly how to do this and make his point. I begged John. I begged him to let me back into the group. They were getting ready to go on tour with Jill. I sobbed, I pleaded, and he said, 'No! It's just too hard to work with you Mich. It's just too emotional. You cause too many problems. This is what Denny and Cass want — it's just not me. You know you betrayed Cass and you've caused nothing but pain for Denny.'

"I always thought that it was very unfair that I was fired. I felt that Denny was as responsible as I was. Denny was very upset about it. He was really caught between a rock and a hard place. He knew that John's position was, 'Hey, look, you want to sing in a group with Michelle Phillips — be my guest. You want to sing in a group with me, the one who writes all the material, the one who arranges all the material, the one who does all the business, then you stay with me. You make your choice.'

"Off they went. They did Forest Hills with Jill and then they played Denver and then Phoenix. They did three dates with her. I spoke to John, on the road, the whole time.

"'How are things going?'

"'Things are going pretty well, we're doing fine.'

"But I could tell things weren't really fine. They had some problems at Forest Hills with people screaming, 'Where is Michelle.' They didn't even bother introducing Jill. I'm not sure what they were trying to do — slip her in and see if maybe people wouldn't notice. We look very much alike. She wore her hair the same way I did, she was blond, blue-eyed, and she sang well. She really did. She certainly sang as well as I did."

As photographer Guy Webster explains, the firing of Michelle caused a significant problem on the cover of the second self-titled album. Michelle's image had to be removed and replaced with a photograph of Jill. "I was traveling with the group," Webster recalls, "going to Arizona or New Mexico on a bus, going from one gig to another. They knew I had to shoot an album cover. But no one wants to shoot an album cover; it's so important that it's almost frightening. We were traveling on the bus and finally there's a spot. Let's shoot. We're out in the middle of nowhere and there is this deserted house and an empty window. I had the group get into the window. It was very graphic, and we all loved the cover. Everybody unanimously loved it and knew this was the second cover. This was the next important cover. We even did a mezzotint screen over the cover and gave it a sense of artistic class or touch.

"We get back to Los Angeles, and there's the major break up of the group. Michelle is leaving and they're hiring Jill Gibson, who's a good singer but not of the caliber of the rest of the group. A very beautiful girl. She came to my studio in Beverly Hills at the time and I photographed her pretty much in the same position that Michelle had been in. Stripped her and etched her into the photograph. It's a classic because it worked so well that you couldn't tell she wasn't actually at the photo shoot in the beginning. I spent days shooting the group with the new singer and we had some fabulous photographs, some really classic rock'n'roll photographs. None of which can be used today because of Jill leaving the group. One of them is a beautiful album that came out with Jill and then was pulled off the racks. I don't know how many, maybe ten or twenty thousand were sold with that old cover. It would really be a wonderful cover to have today."

John soon forgave Michelle and welcomed her back into the band, as she remembers. "They were flying back from Phoenix and John called me one morning. 'Why don't you meet me at the airport when we come in?'

"'Okay, I'll be there.'

"I met them at the airport. Cass and Denny got off and got into their limo. They just kinda said, 'Hi.' That was all. Then Lou and Jill got into their limo and they left.

"John got into the limo with me and I knew right then that whatever had happened, I had been forgiven. I knew then, without a word being spoken, that I was back in the group. That was that."

Following their reconciliation and the re-uniting of the band, resulting in the recording of *Dancing In The Streets*, John and Michelle moved into a house in Bel Air which would soon become the party palace of Hollywood. "When the money started coming in, John and I went house hunting. We knew we wanted to live in Bel Air, so we thought the best way to do it was to just drive around and see what was available. We saw a 'For Sale' sign at 783 Bel Air Road. It said, of course, to call the agent. Well, we couldn't do that so we hopped the fence. It was a beautiful Tudor mansion. It was really cute. It belonged to Jeanette MacDonald, concert singer and leading lady of the 1930s, and her husband Gene Raymond. We peeked in the windows and saw the pub, living room, and kitchen — just a beautiful old house. It had been built in 1932. We decided this was the house of our dreams. We made an offer — the asking price was $225,000, but an offer of $150,000, with a down payment of $90,000 was accepted — and we were in within a month."

John and Michelle soon gained a reputation for throwing lavish parties. Hollywood casting director Michael McLean was one of the frequent guests. "John and Lou Adler used to trade very exotic gifts. Lou had gifted John with a pair of peacocks that were fabulous. They would wander the grounds. Off the living-room balcony, you would see this pair of peacocks fanning their tails into the sunset and flying up into the trees.

"John would hold court and people would come by. He threw fabulous parties and they were the parties to go to and be seen at. The who's who of both music and the motion picture industry were on the guest list and usually showed up. There was a lot of fun in those days. John was this kind of Svengali character."

The only thing different about John when former New Journeyman Marshall Brickman visited him in his Bel Air splendor was his lifestyle, he recalls. "John always had a certain style, a certain seductive, intelligent, southern kind of thing. Not deep South, just Virginia. When I first knew John he was living with Michelle in a one-half room apartment in The Village. It was a walk-up with a bedroom that was literally almost not big enough to hold a bed and a tiny fireplace. A real old Village apartment.

"The next time I saw him he was living in Jeanette MacDonald's house that looked like an enormous cuckoo clock, on two acres, with an enormous pool, pool house, steam rising off the pool and peacocks. But he was exactly the same. He lived in the apartment in The Village with the same effect and personal style that he grew into in L.A. It's almost as though the backdrop grew to accommodate his personal style."

An invitation to one of John and Michelle's celebrated parties was eagerly sought. There were no rules, no restrictions, as John Stewart of the Kingston Trio observed. "I remember going to this great party. It was an astounding party. They wouldn't let Peter Sellers in — it was too crowded. John had come to that stage. Mia Farrow was in the kitchen. It was the elite of Hollywood.

"Lou Adler and I'd go off into John's studio and he'd sit and play me things. It was more money that either of us ever had seen, and John was able to accept it like, 'Yeah! This is right! This is what I am making.' John was very Rudyard Kipling — walk with the kings and not lose the common touch. It was really John. John had that rare ability to be able to be on the same level as anyone he was with, whether it was Roman Polanski or the guy from the corner. The brightest guy I think of that whole era was John Phillips.

"That's when our friendship started to tear at the seams, because of what was going on. I was not that comfortable with all that fame, what they were in to and the life style. I remember going to Whisky A Go Go. I think I went to see Buffalo Springfield. I kept looking at John — this whole new facade of John Phillips. I just couldn't get used to it. He looked at me as if he had no idea who I was. It was like, 'This is me, you know.'"

Joe Cocker, whose Mad Dogs and Englishmen tour established his reputation as a hard-drinking, tough-singing star, has vivid memories of partying with John. "I do remember going to this party. I just knew John very loosely around Hollywood. I remember seeing a mound of blow on this mirror, in the middle of the room, and everyone just casually going up with matchbook covers and just tooting it and wondering whether I was allowed to, sort of, do it. I also remember chatting, in front of a TV, with Peter Lawford, the late actor, watching King Kong and just being generally blown away by the atmosphere. It seemed to me that this sort of thing just happened there every night and it was no big deal to them. But, to me, it was quite a number."

John's sister Rosie also witnessed the seemingly perpetual party in Bel Air when she was invited to attend The Mamas and The Papas concert at the Hollywood Bowl, the concert which fulfilled part of John's promise to Cass, Denny, and Michelle. "John pre-paid first-class tickets for my mother, me, and my children on TWA. I hadn't flown in a long time, and I don't think that my mother had flown since they had bi-planes. We arrived and got into a limousine which had *If You Go To San Francisco . . . Wear Flowers In Your Hair* playing on the radio. Scott McKenzie was singing it. It was a song my brother had written. They drove us up to his big house in Bel Air. That night John was having a concert at the Hollywood Bowl and a big party.

"I had never seen Southern California, never seen Los Angeles. Frankly, I was totally overwhelmed. Here was this gorgeous house, in Bel Air, that had been Jeanette MacDonald's house. It was like a huge fantasy place to go looking around and seeing all these little drawers that she had labeled for gray and pink gloves.

"By limousine we went over to the Hollywood Bowl. Our seats were right up at the front. We had box seats. My mother was there, Susie was there with Jeff and Laura and all my children. Jimi Hendrix was the opening act and he was going through his whole routine of beating up his guitars and everything. The audience was just milling in, and looking for their places to sit. Nobody was paying any attention to Jimi Hendrix. He was not a big name, at that point. He was quite annoyed and would turn his back to the audience. It was an uncomfortable feeling.

"Then Scott McKenzie came on and sang. They had flown in thousands of orchids, from Hawaii, and threw them out to the audience.

"The Mamas and the Papas came on. They had these gorgeous costumes. It was just like a fairy tale thing.

"Afterwards, we were zipped out by limousine and back to John's house in Bel Air. He had this monstrous party. I met Steve McQueen, who stood there and told me what a genius my brother was and what a new thing he was to the music world . . . I felt this was Hollywood. I remember thinking, here I am. Early today, I was in Alexandria, Virginia, and here I am talking to Steve McQueen who was one of my heroes, especially one of my mother's heroes. She loved his television program (*Wanted Dead or Alive*). Lee Majors was there. Some famous actor was being carried out by two people. He had too much to drink.

"Jimi Hendrix came in with two gorgeous blonds, one on each arm. The Mamas and The Papas, of course, were there — Cass, Michelle, John, and Denny.

"The place was just packed, it was an enormous house. Everywhere

I looked I saw people that were well known. I was trying to be very blasé and like I was used to this — this happened to me every day. It didn't. It was my first introduction to Hollywood and it was on a grand scale that night.

"After John and Michelle got so much money, so quickly, from the albums of The Mamas and The Papas, suddenly there were matching cars, enormous paintings being bought. Things from all over — from every auction house in town and every antique place in town — adorned every room. Interior decorators were re-doing everything.

"I remember the swimming pool. The backyard was terraced and Jeanette MacDonald had a stable there. John made that into an echo room when he finally put in his recording studio at the house. Down this winding terrace there was a very large guest house. I went down there and we were all going to go swimming. In the pool were all these sealed up bottles of Crown Royal floating around in the pool, obviously with liquor still in them. I asked John, who was showing me the property, why he'd have bottles floating in the pool. 'I like to have the stuff being the same temperature as my body in the water.' The bottles were floating in the pool so he could take a sip of warm whisky while the air was cold around him. At the time I thought it was very decadent. He had cases of Crown Royal. That was his exclusive drink after he got money.

"I never knew much about drugs. I didn't personally see any drugs but I heard stories of pillowcases full of marijuana at that time, but it was all low key. They just didn't talk to me about it because I was kind of square. I heard different stories, from different people, about Cass having a drug problem and that was giving them a lot of problems with their rehearsals and things like that.

"John and Michelle were constantly chipping away at each other. I thought, at the time, it's a shame because it is breaking up the group."

John's old friend Bill Cleary also was witness to the Bel Air parties. "There were drugs around the house, but John was really down on anything heavy, like morphine. There was one woman, named Willow. We found her in a club called Climax. She came to the house and stayed around for a few days. I was in the bathroom and I found a vial. I took it to John.

"'What's this? Where did you get it?'

"'I found it in the back bathroom.'

"'Willow must be shooting up.'

"'Guess so.'

"'Let's get her out of here.'

"John didn't want to have anything to do with that — nothing at all. He would draw the line on hard drugs. He might do coke, and weed, just the sociable stuff, and not to any degree. He wouldn't shoot, nothing like that. He didn't like it and didn't want to be around anybody who did."

John and Michelle were not the only members of the band to gain notoriety for their hospitality, as MacKenzie Phillips remembers. "We were at Cass Elliot's house. I was six years old. George Harrison, Paul McCartney, my dad, Denny, and Cass were the only people I can remember being there. There was lots of music and the people were playing and I guess smoking dope — doing whatever they were doing. I was a little kid but I knew who The Beatles were.

"Paul McCartney is saying to me, 'Go on luv', get up and dance. No one will notice.'

"I say, 'No! no! no!'

"Finally I got up. I was doing the twist and everyone looked at me and started laughing. I started crying. He took me over to a big hammock. He was holding me in the hammock. I was asleep, a six-year-old girl, asleep in Paul McCartney's arms. That is something that I will never forget. I spent time with Paul McCartney."

Scott McKenzie also remembers meeting Paul McCartney while visiting with John. "This was before I recorded *San Francisco*. John and I had gone our separate ways. We have a habit of doing that regularly. We joined back up again and were looking for a recording project and I was playing in a lot of Mamas and Papas sessions. We were always sort of like a tribe. That was the term they used then. We still are — I call us The Traveling Rehab Circus.

"I was hanging out at John's house a lot and Paul McCartney came over. He ended up staying all night. This was a time when The Beatles visited L.A. We were sitting around playing guitars. I remember Michelle had bought a cello and was taking lessons. Paul picked up the cello and within half an hour he was playing bass on it — that man is from a different planet.

"The Beatles were staying over in Laurel Canyon, which is a few miles east of Bel Air, I was driving back, so I gave Paul a ride. There was this girl whom Paul had met at John's house. She left with Paul and they were sitting in the back seat.

We stop to get gas, *Strawberry Fields Forever* is playing on the radio, and I look at the attendant. I wanted to say, 'Come here a second.' This is just about eight months before SERGEANT PEPPER'S LONELY HEARTS CLUB BAND came out. They were at the pinnacle of their success. I thought I should have done that for the guy pumping gas. He would have loved that — but I didn't.

"I drove them home and Paul gets out and the girl gets in the front seat. I say, 'Well goodnight,' and Paul looks at me kind of funny. He gets back in the car, so I drove to the girl's house and Paul got out with her.

"He pokes his head back in the car and says, 'What do you do?'

"'Well, I sing, play, I'm trying to record.'

"'Oh, alright. Good meeting you.'

"A little less than a year later I had the record *San Francisco* and I was in England at this club where all the rock people used to go. Paul came in one night and he goes, 'So you got yourself a hit record. Huh?'"

San Francisco (Be Sure To Wear Flowers In Your Hair), written by John Phillips and recorded by Scott McKenzie, entered the charts in 1967 and rose to Number 4 in the USA on May 6th and Number 1 in England, holding that position for four weeks. The song defined "Flower Power" and became the anthem for the "Summer of Love" which culminated in the Monterey Pop Festival, organized by John Phillips and Lou Adler. Despite their "internal problems," The Mamas and The Papas would hold together through 1967, winning the Grammy Award for Best Contemporary Rock and Roll Group Performance for *Monday, Monday*, as John had forecast, recording two more albums, DELIVER and FAREWELL TO THE FIRST GOLDEN ERA, and releasing the hit singles *Creeque Alley* and *Safe In My Garden*.

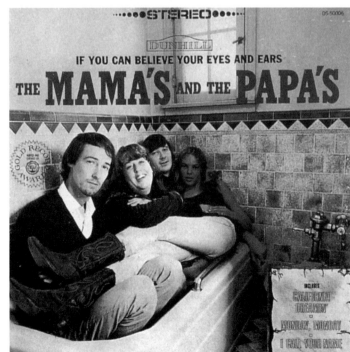

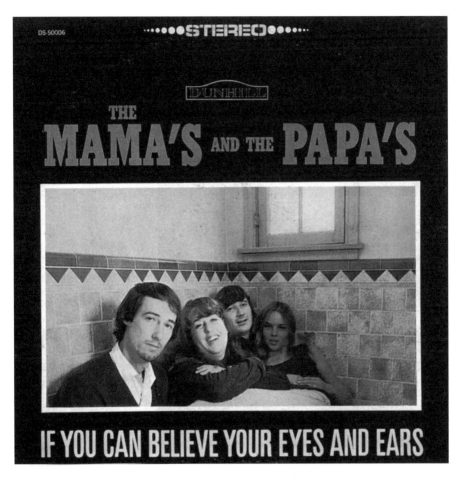

The playful and irreverent original cover for The Mamas and The Papas'
first album was revised through two additional releases to remove bathroom
fixtures which apparently offended 'good taste'.
(Album photo by Guy Webster)

The cover art and publicity photos for their second album were revised to show Jill Gibson in Michelle's place after she was briefly 'fired' from the band. (Photos by Guy Webster)

THE MAMAS & THE PAPAS

BE SURE TO WEAR FLOWERS IN YOUR HAIR

San Francisco (Be Sure To Wear Flowers In Your Hair)

If you're going to San Francisco
Be sure to wear flowers in your hair
If you're going to San Francisco
You're going to meet some gentle people there . . .
All across the nation
Such a strange vibration
People in motion
There's a whole new generation . . .

(John Phillips, ASCAP)

One of John Phillips' most influential achievements was organizing the Monterey International Pop Festival in June 1967 with Lou Adler, Michelle, and a small cast of investor-performers. Although Denny was not involved in the organization of this ground-breaking event — indeed, he almost missed the performance on stage by The Mamas and The Papas — he recalls the genesis of the idea. "Cass and David Crosby came up with an idea for a pop festival. . . some place. They were talking about getting all the groups together. John and Michelle got hold of the idea with Lou and started doing something about it. Cass and David were saying, 'Well my dad's got a barn. I'll get some lights and we can put a play on.' John's going, 'Well wait a minute — a pop festival . . . uh huh!'

"The grand scheme formed and he, Lou, and Michelle started calling everybody in the world. They got offices on Sunset Boulevard. It started to turn into this thing and I said, 'I think I'm going now. I won't go to the office, hang out, make phone calls, and set up this pop festival.' I said, 'I'll be there. Just let me know when you want me for a performance. That's all I want to be involved in this. I'll back you a hundred percent. If anybody asks me, I'll say it's going to be a wonderful venture, but I can't get involved.'

"I left. I went back to St. Thomas where I have lots of old friends. This thing with the eternal triangle was a little too new. Oh! Nothing's happened, let's press on. I took my heart off my sleeve, out of my chest, and threw it on the ground. Michelle came back because he wanted her back. Jill Gibson — or whoever it would have been — would not have made it. The Mamas and the Papas would have died of its own slow death. She came back and they tried to reconcile. Then the pop festival, then the baby came along. It still didn't hold the marriage together. They still split up."

Many fans and music historians debate whether the three-day Monterey Pop Festival, which ran from June 16-18, 1967, was more influential on the course of pop culture than Woodstock two years later, but no one questions that Monterey was better organized and better produced. Much of the credit for its success is a direct result of John's organizational skills. As John explains, "Monterey was set up as a non-profit organization with a steering committee of three and a nine-person board of governors — John Lennon, Paul McCartney, Simon and Garfunkel, and Terry Melcher (Doris Day's son) — some very nice people. Everyone put up ten thousand dollars for seed money. We got our money back, out of the first receipts. All the rest went to scholarships, ghetto workshops for guitar players, and things like that."

Working side-by-side with John to make the Monterey Pop

Festival a resounding success — making pop culture history — had a pacifying effect on their marriage, Michelle observes. "The Monterey Pop Festival was such an incredible success that no one could have known then what we know now. We didn't know that it would become a historical landmark in music, even though that's the way John talked about it as we were putting it together. He saw it as something extremely positive, unique, in the sense that we were bringing together a very diverse group of artists who would never ordinarily perform on the same bill together. It was reflective of the entire music scene. We had Otis Redding, who had never performed to a white hippie audience — ever. It brought together Ravi Shankar, The Who, Buffalo Springfield, The Grateful Dead, Big Brother & The Holding Company with Janis Joplin, Jimi Hendrix, Jefferson Airplane, and Simon and Garfunkel, to name a few. It was a very diverse group of artists and it was a great idea.

"It wasn't John's idea — it was Alan Pariser's idea. He came to Cass with it and then Cass said, 'We want to talk to John.' I remember Allan Pariser and Benny Shapiro came to John and Lou and said, 'We've got this idea. We can make a lot of money. We'll get all these artists together and we'll have a pop festival.' John and Lou wanted to get rid of Benny Shapiro because they didn't want him involved in the project, but they made Allan Pariser one of the organizers of the festival, then they went to work.

"It was great fun. We'd get up in the morning and go to the office, which was a very new experience. I worked on the program — getting businesses to buy ads — and John and Lou worked on the groups. It was a very posh affair — anything John or Lou did was a very posh affair. I remember we had cracked crab at the buffet and French champagne. It was a very classy three days. Everyone was put up at the best hotels. They were flown in by private jet or they were flown in first class. They were all treated like John and Lou treated themselves.

"Who knew Janis Joplin and Jimi Hendrix then? They were virtually unknown. I'd never even heard of Janis Joplin, let alone heard her sing. I'd never heard of Jimi Hendrix. They left you sitting there with your mouth hanging open because they were so new, so innovative. You just could look at these people and say, 'This time next year these people are going to be big stars.' We didn't know then that it would be remembered and thought of as one of the great pop festivals of all time."

Scott McKenzie's hit single, *San Francisco (Be Sure To Wear Flowers In Your Hair)*, which became the anthem of the flower power movement, also worked very well, as John intended, to convince everyone of the gentle nature of the people who would be attending the Monterey Pop Festival. Scott explains how it all went down. "John did write it specifically for me, mainly because during the time of the negotiations for the Monterey Pop Festival, John and Lou were having meetings with very concerned and somewhat frightened townspeople. They weren't sure they wanted the Monterey Fair Grounds invaded by long-haired people. They were sure they would destroy their property. John and Lou were in the process of trying to assure them that precautions would be taken.

"We had been looking for a song and I said, 'John, I can't write this right now. Why don't we do a song that is aimed at the young people who will be arriving in California by the thousands. Let them know that, if they come, they should be peaceful about it and not make enemies.'

"We talked it over for a couple of weeks and he sat down and wrote *San Francisco* one afternoon. We had no idea that it would become such an international hit. It still is. When we go to Europe, the Orient, or South America people want to hear that song, two or three times a show. Even the children of the people who were our age during the '60s want to hear it. He really wrote a classic with that one. I was quite fortunate."

The Festival itself was not without back-stage drama, as John recalls. "Janis Joplin and her band, Big Brother & The Holding Company, had done *Ball And Chain* that afternoon and they had done it so beautifully. No one had really heard her sing outside of San Francisco before her appearance at Monterey. They were a local act, which was the idea of the festival, to bring internationally known acts and acts that were known in their own area who had the potential to go international and give them exposure — let everyone see them work together and compare. Janis was just spectacular.

"I said, 'Do you want to go on tonight, too?'

"She went, 'Oh God! I'd love to go on tonight too — are you kidding?'

"She came back about an hour later. She was crying.

"'What's wrong?'

"'Our manager won't let me go on unless I make a new deal with him.'

"'You've got to be kidding?'

"'No.'

"He wanted to re-negotiate the deal with Janis and all of his acts — Quick Silver, The Grateful Dead, and a bunch of San Francisco acts — so as to get part of the record and movie receipts.

"I just absolutely said, 'No!' I refused to do it. 'I'm not going to cut a special deal for you guys.'

"'Well, Janis can't go on.'

"'Okay, Janis can't go on.'

"She's in tears, wanting to go on so bad.

"'You tell her she can't go on and watch yourself lose a client.'

"'Mmmmmmmmm. Yeah! Maybe we could work something out so she could go on.'

"We worked something out which didn't concern money or anything like that. It was more of a meeting of minds. She went on and killed them again that night. She was wonderful."

True to his word, Denny arrived back in Los Angeles the day of the scheduled performance by The Mamas and The Papas. "The day of the performance, I arrive in L.A. I got my car at eight o'clock in the morning, and I thought 'What's the big thing? I'll drive up. It's a nice drive up the coast highway.' Of course, it takes eight hours to drive up the coast. I got there forty minutes before show time.

"Michelle is screaming, ranting, having seizures, 'He's not going to make it. We're going to be the laughing stock.' Somehow I got a sticker and passed the police lines. I arrived backstage and parked the car somewhere. There was a cop, the size of a mountain. He says, 'You can't come in here.' He had flowers and incense in his helmet.

"'Thank you. I'm in the right place.'

"As the cop is turning around to give me a 'you can't come in here' look, some freak comes over and says, 'Hey man! You want some! Try this. Oh you need some of this.' Speed was everywhere. The cop just turned around, looked away, and started talking to somebody else like, 'I don't see this.'

"On stage was The Who. I didn't know The Who destroyed everything within reach when they were finishing their act. How do you follow that act? They were destroying the stage. 'I'm going, 'Oh shit! Now I've made this trip for nothing — there's nothing left. I can't go on stage, there's nothing left.'

"I think it was D.A. Pennebaker who was running around grabbing his microphones and cameras. I went down to the back room and there is this pile of smoke coming up. You'd get high just breathing through the stairwell. Everyone went, 'Oh, he's here.' Then we went on. I came, did my show. They had been through 'D' Day. The next morning, I went back to L.A."

D.A. Pennebaker was hired to direct the cinema verité feature which hopefully would capture, not only the performances, but the theme and spirit of the festival. "I got a call asking me if I was interested in doing a concert film. I said I was interested in talking about it, so I met with John and Lou. They decided to do it and originally it was proposed as an ABC-TV show.

"John and Lou had arranged to get Brian Wilson's eight track, which I think is the first time that anybody had used an eight track on a concert. We had to figure out how to get a quick mix down and also put some kind of sync signal on there, but that's easy. John and Lou had really set it up so well. The thing was so incredibly put together. The problem I had was how to have it kind of free-flowing.

"We had never done a concert film but we had done some events. We got film makers, actually, most of them were people that worked with us. I'd say they were more musicians than cameramen. But they were film makers. They knew how to make a film. We kind of turned them loose and let them do anything that they wanted to over the three days with the understanding that when people performed, we'd fall into certain positions, but, within those positions, there was no direction — people shot whatever.

"The whole thing was sort of a constant event. It was just kind of an amazing ongoing thing. Some of the music was fantastic. I'd heard the others before, but I had never heard Jimi Hendrix, or seen him really perform like that.

"The whole thing was like running a race. Your vision gets a little clouded. You don't really see everything. You're just kind of moving through it. It was a watershed moment in the '60s when people really thought everything was kind of possible. People like Otis Redding came there because he thought that the whites would stop sopping up the best of black music and putting it on as their own.

"I think the one thing we learned at Monterey was, film is the cheapest thing you have, even though it's expensive to process. At Monterey we just imagined that we would somehow get one song. There were so many groups, there was no way you could envision using all the groups. In an effort to economize, we were only going after one song. If I had to do it again, I would probably shoot almost everything that everybody did.

"I'm really a great fan of John's. I like him a lot. We're very good friends and I prize his friendship greatly. He's been through a lot of very bad times, but he has an indomitable kind of spirit. Of course, I really like the Indian in him. I like that half-crazed, wonderful readiness to climb any mountain that looks intriguing — musically he's fantastic.

"You keep going back to those times — or icons — and try to find out what went wrong or what went right."

John's euphoria at the success of the Monterey Pop Festival and the accolades he and Michelle received for their untiring work in making it a success were dampened by his first wife's decision to sue for support. The papers were served to him during the festival. As Susie Phillips explains, "Once we were divorced, or even separated, there was not a penny that came from John's pocket. I had the two kids and I was having one hell of a rough time. Although I was educated, I didn't seem to be educated in anything — typing or basic skills. I could write so Rosie got me a job in the Pentagon as a file clerk for . . . I think it was about $3,600 a year. How can you support two kids on that?

"John agreed to send money, but I knew him well enough to think, 'When he gets it, I'll get it. When he doesn't, I'll make it myself.' I went to an attorney, finally. My family convinced me — go get him!

"I spoke with one of John's old buddies who had become an attorney. He tried to find John and finally he found him, and served him papers, at the Monterey Pop Festival.

"I didn't call John, John called me because he knew, damn well, he was in for trouble. That was when he said he would send me five thousand dollars. God! that sounded like heaven — that sounded like five million dollars, at the time. Through his accountant, Don Sterling, I got the check. I went to the bank. I was so thrilled with it. I gave Rosie a thousand dollars because she had been helping me out. I don't know what I would have done without her or John's mother (Den). They both just kept me and the kids, alive. I figured I owed them more than that because I loved them both so much. I still love Rosie — she's my best friend. I gave Den five hundred and the rest, I put in the bank.

"I thought, 'Boy, am I sitting pretty.' It was nothing to John at the time. He could just flip it out of his pocket. It helped. I guess he just thought, 'That will shut Susie up for a while.'

"It did."

Much to the surprise of their fans, John called a press conference in early September to announce that The Mamas and The Papas were breaking up, the same week they were booked to appear on the top-rated *Ed Sullivan Show* in New York, a performance John fondly recalls, especially the fun Cass had at the expense of Ed Sullivan. "Cass really had Sullivan's number. On a one-to-one basis she had fear of no one. She could talk to anybody and just out do them, out wit them, out smart them, anything she wanted to do.

"Sullivan was sort of like a puppet. She would just kid him unmercifully during rehearsals. It was like, 'Can't remember your lines, right, Ed? Shoe. Think shoe, Ed. Think really big shoe.'

"Ed came out and said — he always interviewed you for a moment after your song — 'Well, how are you fellows doing?'

"Cass says, 'We're not fellas, Ed.'

"Then Ed goes 'mmmmmmmmm.' His mouth didn't move at all, the lips stay frozen, solid. Cass gave him a kiss on the cheek — she was outrageous."

Michelle looks back on the Sullivan shows she did with The Mamas and The Papas as a mirror of her professional development. "The Sullivan shows were interesting. As I look back and watch them, I see how my development was very evident on those tapes. In the first couple of tapes I am very withdrawn and shy. The more shows we did I'm out there throwing balls at Ed Sullivan. I've loosened up quite a bit. John, Cass, and Denny used to berate me all the time because

I wouldn't speak on stage, but you can see as I became more confident, I started to horse around a little bit more on stage.

"One show I remember in particular was the Rogers and Hart special we did with Quincy Jones, The Supremes, and Petula Clark. It was a big NBC Special and it was the first and probably only special we ever did. The Supremes, at that time, were very different from what they finally became, which was a glittery Las Vegas act. They were still these little girls from Detroit who were big stars but weren't worldly in any sense. Cass put a stick of incense on their dressing room door, then we waited for them to come down stairs.

"We heard one of them say, 'Who put that pump on our door? The Mamas and The Papas put that pump on our door.'

"They were very suspicious of this new group, with hair down to here and the girls didn't wear shoes — one girl was this big and the other one so skinny the wind could blow her over. The tall guy wore a beard and a hat. They were very suspicious of this new look. They were still into that glittery New York look. They all wore the same thing. They just didn't like us at all. They certainly didn't like the idea we stuck this piece of incense on their door. They weren't sure what that meant and they didn't like it."

Denny recalls another time when Ed Sullivan froze on camera. "Oh God! Poor Ed. I guess he had just been doing the show so long. We did the show two or three times. Sullivan was supposed to walk up and say, 'Well, what we hear is that you kids are breaking up. That's not true is it? It's not really true that you're breaking up? You're just going on a sabbatical, some place, isn't that right?' That was what he was supposed to say. He did very well in rehearsal.

"I was supposed to answer him and say, 'No. It's not true. We're going to Majorca. We're going to find whatever.

"Show starts, red light. He walks up. He just stood there. What am I supposed to do? It's Ed Sullivan. He's frozen right in front of thirty million people — tape's rolling.

"I did both sides of the conversation. 'Well, Ed I suppose you heard that we're breaking up. Well, we're not breaking up.' I was like a dog passing razor blades. We never did get to Majorca."

The announcement of the break up of The Mamas and Papas did indeed prove to be premature, though they did not travel to Majorca, instead sailing for England on 29 September 1967. With a baby on the way, John and Michelle hoped that the trip might help their marriage and the band, as John explains. "We thought we'd try to regroup in Paris for a while. Just live there and see how things went. We got as far as England. It was just evident that we all had burned ourselves out emotionally, artistically, psychologically, and physiologically. We were toast. The one nice thing that happened was we crossed the Atlantic on the S.S. *France* and everyone had to dress in first class for dinner every night with tuxedos and gowns."

Michelle picks up the story, including what happened on the brief stop-over in Boston. "We made a stop in Boston. John and Denny got off the ship and scored some pot — a big bag of it. We knew that there was no possible way to smoke it all, so Denny cleaned it. Cass and I put it in baggies and sewed them into the lining of our coats. The first night that we came into the dining room everyone stood up and gave us a standing ovation. It was probably more for the clothes we were wearing than anything else. We were all decked out.

"We knew that we were supposed to dress for dinner on a ship. So we were completely decked out in our finest Indian robes and Nehru suits, and what have you. We sat at the Captain's table and it was absolutely terrific."

The trip started out on a high note, so to speak, but by mid-Atlantic disaster struck, as John relates. "We were watching *Doctor Zhivago* and were in mid-ocean when one of the stabilizers on the ship went out. The screen was rocking back and forth and we were all getting seasick. It was stormy, very stormy. It was early winter and this is sort of a bad time to cross. The other stabilizer started going from over-work. A smell started coming through the ship and then the loud-speaker came on and said, 'Will all passengers please go to their rooms and put their life jackets on.'

"We thought, 'Hey, we're out in the middle of nowhere, Jack!' We went to our rooms and suddenly there is this huge scream out of Cass's room.

"I yell out the door, 'What's wrong?'

"'It's not big enough to fit around me. I'm going to drown — I'm going to drown!'

"Denny is very good with his hands. He fashioned two life jackets together and made them fit around her. She was happy then waiting for the ship to sink.

"'I'm in Denny's hands now, fine, fine, everything's fine.'

"We landed at Portsmouth. They were taking passports as you got off. They took Cass's passport, but they wouldn't give it back. I was next. They looked at mine, put it aside and said, 'Would you mind sitting over here. I went and sat with Cass. Then Denny and Michelle. We were all sitting in a line of chairs.

"Cass said to me, 'What am I going to do?'

"'What do you mean?'

"'I've got about a quarter pound of grass in each bra cup.'

"You couldn't really notice on Cass.

"'What are you going to do? Yeah!'

"Michelle said, 'Me, too.'

"Obviously we were in some kind of trouble. Every other passenger had left the ship.

"'Pretend you're sick then flush it down the toilet.'

"So, Cass over-dramatizes — 'Oh, oh' — falling to the floor, writhing and rolling across the floor.

"'I'm ill! I'm nauseous! I'm going to vomit!' She ran to the ladies room."

Michelle again picks up the story. She is five months pregnant, not thinking too straight and nearly in a panic.

"She's gone and gone and gone — she's gone for a long time. Finally John says, 'Michelle go to the bathroom and see if she's alright.'

"I get to the bathroom and open the door. Cass is on her hands and knees. There is pot from one end of the bathroom to the other. She's trying to scoop it up and flush it down the toilet. It won't flush down the toilet because it's all loose. She's crying — she's totally hysterical. She's got pot all over her hands. She's got it all over her hair. It couldn't have been a worse situation."

John didn't have to be told the situation was serious. "About ten minutes later they still hadn't come back and the custom officials were getting very nervous. They said, 'We better go check this out.'

"'That's not very gentlemanly. Let me do it. I'll go check and come back with a report.'

"They were very nice. 'Alright, that's fine.'

"The whole ladies room was covered with grass. There's grass on the ceiling, grass on the walls — they're trying to flush it. They didn't know anything about rolling it in toilet paper first, then flushing it.

"So I said, 'Clean yourselves up, go back out, and stall them for ten minutes. I'll get rid of this.'

"So, I locked the door to the ladies room. People are pounding on the door, trying to get in. I'm scraping marijuana off the walls — flushing it down the toilet.

"We got away with that."

The calamities continued, taking on the aura of a Monty Python sketch as Cass was arrested dockside for stealing blankets the last time she was in London. "There is a constable ready to arrest Cass," Michelle recalls. "He won't tell her why she's being arrested.

"John says, 'If you won't tell her why, then she won't go with you.'

"The constable says, 'We're definitely taking her in,' and he turned to Cass.

"'Cass don't go with them. If they won't tell you why they are arresting you, you don't have to go with them,' orders John.

"'This is Great Britain, sir, and we have the right to take her into custody. We don't have to tell you why we're taking her into custody.'

"'She will not go with you.'

"We were being met by the Rolling Stones, with a string of Rolls Royces, so I said, 'Cass, that sounds pretty reasonable to me. I wouldn't go with them either.'

"Cass gets into one of the Rolls. I get into the Rolls with her. Cass is in the middle and John and I are flanking her. They put a barricade up to stop the cars from moving anywhere.

"Within a few minutes there is a huge matron, I mean, I have never seen a woman soooooo big.

"Cass says, 'No!'

"The woman reaches in and then this tug of war ensues. I'm holding onto Cass, John's holding on to Cass — but this woman won the tug of war. She was so big. She drags Cass out of the Rolls, puts the cuffs on her, and takes her away. I had whipped myself into such a frenzy that I went up to this woman and I hit her in the mouth — I hit this matron in the mouth. I don't know what was possessing me at this moment.

"She still had hold of Cass. She just looked at me and screamed,

'I'll come back and get you for assault.' She never did. They took Cass off to jail, where she spent the night.

"The next morning we went to court and we're all in very, very, bad shape. They dismissed all charges in spite of the fact they had found a big roach and pot cookie in Cass's purse. They gave them back to her before she was arraigned.

"On the six o'clock TV news, the four of us are walking down the steps of the court and we see Cass going into her purse. She pulls out this big cookie and we're all eating. She's eating it, I'm eating it, Denny's eating it, and John's eating it. We were eating the evidence because she was certain she was going to be re-arrested on the steps of the court. That, of course, never happened."

John adds another spin to what happened when Cass was arrested and the traumatic impact the events had on the group. "The police are trying to put Cass in handcuffs. Michelle is six months pregnant and Michelle cold cocks this lady cop. It's 'come back for more if you want some more of that' — 19th-century boxing style. They took Cass away after a lot of heated arguments and fighting on the docks. They put her into a police car, took her to a precinct, and charged her with theft.

"We immediately went to an art's supply store and bought placards that said, 'Set Mama Cass free!' The media picked up on it, and suddenly there were like a hundred cameras there. The BBC filmed the whole thing.

"Michelle really had a tough day — fighting the cops and the wash-room scene with the marijuana. She fainted and that was a big thing. 'Pregnant Mama faints while trying to gain the release of a partner.'

"Cass went to court and it was great! The judge finally said, after hearing the evidence, 'I find no reason to hold someone guilty. She made reparations for the blankets and towels and paid the hotel bill. You leave this court as you entered Madam, with your honor unsullied.'

"And, she says 'Thank you, judge,' like one of the Bowery Boys. The whole place broke into applause and the judge banged his gavel.

"We went to the police sergeant's desk to gather her belongings which they had taken away from her at the beginning. We knew she had two hash cookies and a roach in her personal effects. They handed them back to her. We couldn't believe it. We're looking around. This is some kind of a set-up. What's going on?

"I picked up the two cookies and said, 'Hungry Denny?

"'Yeah! I am very hungry.'

"We ate the cookies and I think Cass swallowed the roach. We walked out of there chewing away in front of the media.

"When we got back to the hotel everyone was emotionally upset by everything that had happened — the headlines in the *Daily Mirror*, every day. We had decided to go to Majorca to rehearse. I had leased a house on the far side of the island to see if we could pull it back together again musically — get the muse going again and so forth. I think Michelle and I were the only ones who really thought that this was possible.

"We called a big meeting in the hotel. Cass told me that she wanted to go out on her own and be a solo act. She just felt that things weren't getting any better with the group. She said, 'I hear the sound of a different drum. I'm going to follow it.'"

To add to this cauldron of tension and turmoil, Michelle confessed to John that she was now in love with Lou Adler. With Cass going solo and John and Michelle still involved in their soap opera, The Mamas and The Papas appeared to be through as a group, ready to be consigned to the corridors of memory.

By the time their third and fourth albums were
released, The Mamas and the Papas began to
play with their own image, reversing their name
on "The Papas and The Mamas" and taking
to the Bel Air pool of John and Michelle for
"Deliver." (Album photos by Guy Webster)

129

The Mamas and The Papas
appeared on stage, on record,
and on film at the Monterey
International Pop Festival.

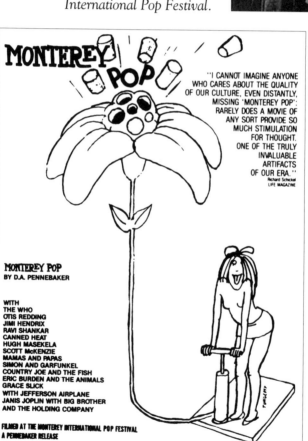

THE MAMAS & THE PAPAS

MAKE YOUR OWN KIND OF MUSIC

Make Your Own Kind Of Music

Nobody can tell ya'
There's only one song worth singin'
They may try and sell ya'
Because it hangs them up to see someone like you
But you've gotta make your own kind of music
Sing your own special song
Make your own kind of music
Even if no one else sings along . . .

(Barry Mann-Cynthia Weil, BMI)

"Cass always wanted to be a soloist," recalls Michelle. "She dreamed of the day that she could get rid of us and go out on her own. She saw herself as a hip Barbra Streisand. That was really the kind of music that appealed to her. She loved the theater. She loved that style of music more than she loved rock, folk, or folk rock. She just wanted to sing.

"There were a lot of people around her who were saying, 'Why do you put up with this? Why do you put up with this nonsense with Michelle, Denny, and John?' We'd just had the Monterey Pop Festival and she had not been a part of it because she didn't want to be a part of it. She wanted to be on the road, making money. Because she didn't write, she didn't have the luxury of having publishing money coming in.

"John, she felt, was out to make a name for himself with the Monterey Pop Festival and Lou, too — Michelle was going along for the ride. Michelle didn't care, she had a lot of money. Together, we did have a lot more money than Cass. She resented that, I think. She felt people were telling her, 'You can be a soloist, you don't need them — that's what you should be aiming at.' Even Dunhill Records was saying it. They were covering their asses all the time. They were telling her, if you want to go out as a soloist and the group breaks up, you have a home right here at Dunhill Records. She knew she had nothing to lose by going out by herself and maybe a lot to gain. I can't really say that I thought Cass was better on her own than she was in the group because I liked The Mamas and the Papas music more than I liked the music that Cass was doing on her own. We just had different tastes."

Cass did record four albums with Dunhill between October 1968 and October 1970 — DREAM A LITTLE DREAM, BUBBLEGUM, LEMONADE AND SOMETHING FOR MAMA, MAKE YOUR OWN KIND OF MUSIC, and MAMA'S BIG ONES. She also began to tour on her own, playing such venues as Caesar's Palace in Las Vegas, as Michelle remembers. "The night that she opened at Caesar's Palace, John, Denny, and I decided to go up and surprise her. She didn't know that we were in the audience, and she said some very nasty things about the group. She was very sick. She was on antibiotics and all sorts of pain killers. She only did the first show and then she canceled because she was so sick.

"She said things and it really hurt our feelings. I thought no matter what has gone down she should still see that The Mamas and The Papas are what brought her to this day and I resented her. I just felt that she should have had better feelings about the group. I don't know how I can say that but I did. I felt that she should have had kinder feelings about the group, at least in public and at least what she said about us in public.

"There was a very strong feeling within the group that whatever happened we kept it to ourselves. Maybe that was one reason it made it so hard because it was almost like we were living a lie, a lot of times. We presented ourselves as this happily married couple and this other couple who adored each other — and we were the best of friends. I don't doubt that it must have been hard to live up to, to try to keep that as our image all the time.

"I still think that it was kind of a rule, that we had, an unspoken rule, that whatever happened within the group we kept to ourselves. Cass wasn't doing that."

Cass's first single, *Dream A Little Dream Of Me*, written by the songwriting team of Wilbur Schwendt/Fabian Andre/Gus Fabian, proved to be her biggest hit. Originally released in April 1968 on the fourth album of The Mamas and The Papas called THE PAPAS AND THE MAMAS PRESENTED BY THE MAMAS AND THE PAPAS, which was recorded in the Bel Air mansion studio, *Dream A Little Dream Of Me* was released as a single in June 1968 with the credit line reading "featuring Mama Cass with The Mamas and The Papas." Clearly, Cass Elliot was reluctant to leave "Mama Cass" behind, despite her desire for a solo career:

Stars shining bright above you
Night breezes seem to whisper 'I love you'
Birds singin' in the sycamore tree
Dream a little dream of me . . .

Famous session guitarist James Burton, who had played with Elvis Presley and Ricky Nelson, worked with Cass and has fond memories of the days he spent in the studio with her. "I would have to say that one of my favorite people in The Mamas and the Papas was Mama Cass. She was such a sweetheart and such a great singer. I worked on a solo album with her. That was fantastic. I put the musicians together for that album. It was so much fun, I ended up playing banjo and practically every string instrument on the album. She was just great! The blend with The Mamas and the Papas, the blend of voices, was just so perfect and beautiful. It was an honor to work with those people."

Two months before the release of THE PAPAS AND THE MAMAS

album Chynna Gilliam Phillips was born on 12 February 1968, an occasion that prompted Michelle to assess the state of her marriage and the state of the band. "There was no question that the group breaking up had a definite affect on our marriage. It became apparent that we had been together for a long time just because of the group. It was getting impossible to write. God knows we turned every disaster into publishing, if we could, and every great thing that happened to us was also turned into publishing. Anything was turned into publishing. After a while the inspiration was just lost, and without the material we really didn't want to record.

"Cass had had her baby and I was pregnant with Chynna and ready to give birth. I really didn't have any interest in writing or recording. After Chynna was born, we weren't on the road and we weren't performing at all. I guess John and I just realized that there wasn't much left."

John agrees there was little inspiration left but cites the root of exhaustion as being the crossed passions of the band members. "It was all the relationships within the group. Like Cass being in love with Denny, Denny being in love with Michelle, and Michelle being in love with Lou. Lou being in love with Jill Gibson, and Jill being in love with Elmer Valentine who owned the Whisky a Go Go and who used to travel with us all the time.

"I was sort of in love with all of them. I didn't know what to do. It was all that tension that wore us out. Everyone always being in love with each other, having affairs and things like that suddenly just wore it all down. That's the way it happened."

Following the release of their single *Safe In My Garden* in June 1968, The Mamas and The Papas finally did disband, leaving as their legacy a remarkable string of hit singles and four albums, recorded in less than three years, songs which continue to define their era three decades later.

A year later in May 1969 John Phillips filed for a divorce from Michelle, and in June he met his third wife, Genevieve Waite. Concerning his break up with Michelle, John comments, "I suppose when someone is twenty-six, twenty-seven, years old, they've formed a lot of their own opinions. I was twenty-six, twenty-seven, and Michelle was seventeen, or eighteen at the start. We'd been crossing state lines, illegally, for years by that time.

"I had grown up. Michelle hadn't really had the chance to grow up, date, go to high school proms and do this kind of stuff. After a person sort of goes through that period, of say sixteen to nineteen, twenty, years old, they are not the same person that they were when they were sixteen. They are not the person that you fell in love with. They are their own person. That's what really happened to us. It's exactly what it was, as a matter of fact.

"She was really getting into political issues, into life, into things that were happening then. Things that I had dealt with years before — there wasn't much room for conversation."

From Capetown, South Africa, Genevieve Waite had immigrated to England, where she worked as a model and competed successfully against 350 other actresses for a part in the film *Joanna*. At the time John and Genevieve met, he was writing music for the 20th Century Fox film *Myra Breckinridge*, starring John Huston, Raquel Welch, and Rex Reed. His song *Secret Places* appears on the soundtrack.

John continued to live the high life, as his old bandmate Marshall Brickman recalls, a lifestyle which almost led to his death at the hands of Charles Manson's followers at Sharon Tate and Roman Polanski's home at 10050 Cileo Drive on August 9, 1969. "I was the head writer for Johnny Carson," Marshall Brickman relates, "and two or three times a year the show would go out to L.A. from New York. I lived two lives. One was living in Gene Autry's Continental Hotel on Sunset Boulevard and I'd drive out to Burbank, write my jokes, and sketches, and immerse myself in the real mainstream popular television culture. In the evening I would get in a rented car and I'd drive out to Bel Air where John had this kind of movable feast, or permanent feast — sort of open house with the big furniture, the brocade walls, and these strange people sort of floating in.

"It was like an aquarium. These people would kind of float through the rooms and I'd come to kind of decompress and to balance the other part of my life. I'd show up or call and say, 'Well, John, what's going on? What's happening tonight in the nether world?'

"That one particular night, John said, 'Well, we have two options.

We can go out to Michael Sarne's, the director, he has a house in Malibu County, and play pool, or we could go up to Sharon Tate's. She's having some people over, up in Benedict Canyon.'

"Now as a gag writer for Carson I read every newspaper and every periodical in the world searching desperately for material. I had read in the L.A. *Times* that the phosphorescent plankton were in that day and apparently this was a thing when colonies of plankton floated in. When the waves broke you'd get an effect like a big neon glow that went along the beach. I'd never seen that.

"I said, 'Well, obviously, we have to go out and see the plankton.' As a result, we didn't go to the scene of mayhem. I went back to the hotel in the middle of the night and left instructions not to send any calls through because I was exhausted.

"The first victim that they found up in Benedict Canyon was an unidentified young man (Stephen Parent) in a rented Ford, which is what I had. My girlfriend — later my wife — heard that. I had told her that we were going to either one of these two places. She was in New York and she heard on the radio what had happened. That cemented our relationship. When I woke up at noon there were a hundred and sixty messages from everybody wanting to know if I had gone over to the party."

John's version of the events is no less lively. "We went out to dinner and I was supposed to go to Sharon's house. There were some messages on my machine saying, 'We're having a party. Come on over.' I had been going there a lot during the summer. Roman had been in England — he was filming some movie. I think it was *Rosemary's Baby*.

For some reason Marshall wanted to go to the ocean, something about how beautiful the sunset was on the Pacific. He talked me out of going to Sharon's house. We took some substances and watched the sun set — little knowing that, at the same time, this massacre was happening up in the Hollywood Hills. The next morning, it was a real shock. This reporter from the L.A. *Times* called. She was the Entertainment Editor.

"'Oh, thank God you're alive.'

"'What do you mean?'

"'They found five, or six, bodies over at Roman Polanski's house. They won't identify the bodies yet because next of kin haven't been notified. We're calling all of their friends. I was hoping you weren't one of them.'

"That's how I first found out about it that morning."

That summer John began work on his first solo album, JOHN, THE WOLF KING OF L.A., released in 1970. "John blew his load on THE WOLF KING album," reports Denny. "That was material that he had lived with for a long time. It took him a long time to get into the studio and record that album. Those songs, the material, the emotion, the lyrical content, the way all the arrangements would have worked in his head were all for the group — I'm sure."

John's opinion of this album in retrospect is equivocal. "THE WOLF KING album is a strange phenomena. Polls, all over the world, still place it in the top one hundred rock albums of all time. Personally, I never liked it. I was in a great depression at the time. It got incredible reviews in *Rolling Stone*, *The New York Times*, different music publications and tabloids."

Even as Cass and John pursued their own recording careers, circumstances were conspiring to re-unite The Mamas and The Papas, as Denny explains. "In my mailbox was a letter from ABC Dunhill Records saying, 'You owe us two hundred and fifty thousand dollars. You haven't given us any product as a member of The Mamas and The Papas and your contractual commitment blah, blah,blah. We're suing you for a few hundred thousand.'

"Oh no! They were suing me for two hundred and fifty thousand. I call everybody.

"'Did you get the letter?

"'Oh yeah. I got one.'

"'I got one.'

"'I got one.'

"Four times two hundred and fifty thousand — that's a million dollars!

"They're suing the group for a million dollars.

"'How do we get out of this?'

"'Give us product.'

"Okay, we'll give you product if this is the last thing we do for you. Let's go in and make an album and get out of all this bullshit."

John wrote new songs for the PEOPLE LIKE US album but calls it a "phantom" album because of the way it was recorded. There were monumental problems. "I remember, very distinctly, when we did the last album, PEOPLE LIKE US — it was a phantom album. I never had all four people in the studio at the same time. I put on Denny's tenor part, and then Cass would come in and sing a lead to that, and Michelle would put on her soprano part. We were so estranged from each other, by that time. We were just doing it as a contractual thing to get out of our contract with ABC Dunhill.

"I was working twenty-four hours a day on this thing to get it over with. It seemed to be never-ending — it went on, and on, and on. Tapes were erased, engineers would make mistakes, microphones wouldn't be on. It was like a ghost was haunting it."

Recording the album wasn't exactly Denny's idea of a good time, either. "Cass had her nurse in the studio with her. Jack Nicholson was coming by to see Michelle. 'Are you through your recording session yet?' John would be blah, blah, blah. Genevieve's at home. I'm living over on Silver Lake with the mother of my first daughter."

After the release of PEOPLE LIKE US in spring 1971, ABC Dunhill Records released The Mamas and The Papas from their contract, much to the relief of everyone in the group, especially John. "Eventually the album came out — listenable but not what we really wanted. I remember Cass turning to me and saying, 'You know, we really created a little gem here with the first four albums that we did. Obviously this fifth one isn't what we want or wanted to do. We were just doing it for business purposes, not for the artistic sake or for personal satisfaction. It was just to get out of contracts. That's why people are acting this way. Why don't we just live with it and just go on and do our separate things?'

"It made a lot of sense to everybody. That was the way to do it."

Michelle still thought the idea of the group getting back together again might work. "I thought, none of us are really doing anything, and if we could get together and put out an album together, it would be great. Maybe we could get back on track. Once again we didn't have any material that we liked. John was writing some stuff that I just didn't like. He was with Genevieve and he seemed to be influenced by a lot of people that I didn't respect. There were things going on which I started to suspect. I kept hearing that they were into drugs. I mean, that they were into serious hard drugs. I never thought that John would be vulnerable to that. I didn't like the people he was hanging out with, they were his best friends.

"The material that came out of that PEOPLE LIKE US album was at best mediocre. It was just a mistake. It was a way to get us out of our contract which was hanging over our heads.

"There was a big change in John. The fact that we weren't all together didn't help matters. It didn't help the sound of the group and it didn't help the whole feeling of the four of us being together. An important element in the group was the relationship between us. I started seeing that John was not productive in the way that he had been in the '60s and we were just trying to beat a dead horse."

During 1971 Cass married Baron Donald von Weidenman, and John and Genevieve began collaboration on an ill-fated musical project they called "Space," which they envisioned as a Broadway production. John was confident that this musical would be the greatest achievement of his career. "That was really fun. It was more fun than work, really. It was disappointing in the fact that I had spent two years writing it, writing all the music for it and the lyrics.

"A fellow named Lenny Holzer was a close personal friend. He wanted to do it as a film. He put a lot of money into it. Ray Stark, a producer, wanted to do it as a film and he put money into it. But it never really seemed to get off the ground. The book was very politically oriented. I took it to New York and we started having backer parties. Genevieve and I would sing the songs and we'd explain the story. We raised money to do the show like that. In a matter of six weeks we had half-a-million dollars to do the show.

"Andy Warhol wanted to produce it, which was great. Andy was like the hero of New York — the great artistic guru and all this. Andy was an absolute genius. If you ever had a crisis in your life you would go to Andy and say, 'Andy these are the facts. What am I supposed to do now?' He'd look at page thirty six and give you the answer. He wrote a book called "Andy Warhol's Philosophy from A to Z."

Andy produced the show, Paul Morrissey directed it. They had made films together but nothing ever musical — nothing that ever required moving the camera. They had made a film called "The Empire State Building," which showed the entrance of The Empire State Building for six hours — people walking in and out of it. "Sleeping" was one of their big ones where a guy is on the couch asleep for four hours and you watch him roll over and snore and scratch himself. The high point is like two-and-a-half hours into the film — a fly lands on his nose. That drew great applause.

"I had meetings with Andy and Paul. I'd walk into his office — or the 'factory' — to discuss script changes, lyric changes, costumes and things like that. I'd cough, and Andy would go, 'Oh, that's great! Leave it in. I love that part. Leave it in.'

"'I just coughed, Andy, that's all I did.'

"'I love it! I love it! Leave that in. Let's put that little cough right over here.'

"Really uncanny to work with him because he was a very strange man. As a matter of fact Andy wore this very strange toupee which was gray, orange, and silver. It finally got so ragged that everyone, all of his friends, chipped in and bought him a new toupee and took the other one away from him."

"He was a wonderful guy."

While her father was exploring the art film world, MacKenzie Phillips was being cast for a role in *American Graffiti*. Following Susie's second marriage, MacKenzie and Jeffrey moved in with John and Genevieve in June of that year. MacKenzie has always had a soft spot for Denny. "Denny was my Dutch uncle," recalls MacKenzie. "When I was dating he would always want to know, 'Who is this young man? What are your intentions.'

"I'd be, 'Denny, come on.'

"Michelle would take me out shopping at Saks Fifth Avenue and stuff like that.

"I have memories, two memories, of Cass, from being on Lear jets with her and in Dad's studio. When I was young, Dad used to come in the middle of the night, pick us up in the Lear, and take us away somewhere. I remember sitting on Cass's lap in the Lear. I also remember in the recording studio, in the attic of Dad's house, sitting on a huge paisley covered pillow — real '60s stuff with purple tassels hanging off.

Cass was trying to teach me to play gin rummy. I just remember this big, warm, funny, crackling kind of a lady. It was a fantasy childhood.

"Dad showed *Monterey Pop* at my tenth birthday party. I was a little hippie kid with a head band, leather fringed vest, and shoes that everybody called Fairchilds — high calf-length moccasin shoes. All the kids were there. Genevieve was there. She was, like, eighteen or something. Just very young and shaky in this little, purple suede mini skirt. I'm going 'mmmmmmmmmmmm. I wonder if I'll get any brothers and sisters from her.' I did and they're great.

"One time I was at Dad's for the weekend and he and Genevieve were out. I was just like around the house and Donovan shows up at the door. I guess I must have been eleven.

"'They'll be back soon.'

"Donovan started playing guitar and singing. I was sliding down the bannister and running around the house. I got him to slide down the bannister with me. Then, I gave hash brownies to Donovan. I didn't know that they were hash brownies. They were in the refrigerator. That was it.

"'Do you want some brownies and milk?'

"We started eating those brownies, then, all of a sudden, like wow!"

"When Dad came home, he asked, "'You guys, you weren't eating *those* brownies, were you?'

"That was a weird thing.

"I was twelve years old, fifth grade, or something, when my acting career started. I was singing in a rock group that we put together. Dad always encouraged all of his children. He gave them space to be what they wanted to be. I don't remember any specifics like you should go into the business or you shouldn't.

"I put this rock group together at school and we played at the Troubadour in L.A. on amateur night. Dad was there. I was twelve years old up there singing rock'n'roll. Songs about prison, smokin' dope, and drinking beer. There was a casting director there who was casting *American Graffiti.*

"'Do you want to be in the movie?'

"'Like, for sure.'

"'Okay.'

"I went out and tried out for the film and that's what happened.

"At that time my relationship with Dad was weekends. We'd go to his house, my brother Jeffrey and I. Donovan would be sitting there or Mick Jagger. Then we'd go home to the Valley — from Bel Air to the Valley. You know, 'Sit up straight at the table and hold your hands.' Then, on weekends it was wow! Wild children. He didn't give us a schedule or specifics until we moved in with him.

"Dad's drug involvement was a very insidious thing. It grew on its own. When you first get kind of caught up in something like that, you don't think of the long term at all. It's the high — that's what it is all about. Dad was always just 'so'. I don't know if he was unaware or didn't worry about what people thought. He always seemed to be in his own space.

"Jeffrey and I moved in with him. I arrived in a taxi, I knocked on the door of this big mansion. He answers the door.

"'Dad, can you pay the cab? I'm moving in.'

"'Uh, uh, uh.'

"'What are the ground rules?' I was twelve, maybe thirteen. I'd already done *American Graffiti*.

"'Okay, let me see. You can never come home in the same clothes you left in. You have to be home by five a.m. One night a week you can stay out all night.'

"Well, you tell that to a thirteen year old, who had just done a hit movie and has her own wing of a mansion — you go nuts.

"Dad and Gen had their wing, I had my wing, and my brother, Jeffrey, had his wing in the house. Dad had a baby blue grand piano in his bedroom. It's hard to talk to someone and have them see what I saw. It was just a fairy tale lifestyle.

"Dad wrote a song about me, *Fairy Tale Girl*. It's accurate. When I moved into the mansion, there were no holds barred. I started hanging out on Sunset Strip and shaved my eyebrows. I could do anything — and I did!"

Michelle is bluntly honest about John's questionable parenting skills. "He's never been a really good father to any of his children, but he is when it's convenient. When it's not convenient, he's not there."

Susie remembers John as being a good father in the early years, but knows when he changed. "When Jeffrey was born, my God, he was his fair-haired boy. He was a wonderful father when Jeffrey was an infant. He really was very careful with him, very caring. Really, a very good husband and father at the time. I think he stopped caring about the children when he met Michelle. I cannot blame it on Michelle because Michelle was pretty good to the kids."

Living in a mansion without rules and in a fairy tale world had its down side. There were problems between MacKenzie and John's third wife Genevieve. "My step-father, my mother's second husband, was Jewish and I started becoming interested in Judaism. Genevieve was South African and she kind of had a semitic problem. One night we were in the basement. Actually it was the ballroom and it had a dance floor. Tibetan murals were painted on the walls. It was built by William Randolph Hearst. There was also a little servant's quarters off to the side. My brother and I decided we wanted to live down there. Genevieve came down and started screaming, 'Liar, liar, liar. You little bitch I'm going to kill you!' She started beating me up so I started punching and kicking. She ripped the Jewish Star of David off my neck and threw it across the room. Then, Michelle came in.

"Michelle was living in the guest house then. So, it was Michelle, John, Genevieve, Jeffrey, Tamerlane, Chynna, Marsia Trinder, and a yippie — first wives, second wives, kids from your first marriage, kids from your second marriage. Michelle came in the middle of this fight. She kicked Genevieve in the shins and threw her over a table. The whole time Genevieve is saying, 'I hate it here, I hate you all. I'm going back to South Africa.' But I love her very much. She was good to me.

"Dad has never got really mad at me. There was a courtyard and one of their bedroom windows was here and mine was on the other side of the courtyard. I remember yelling 'You bitch' at each other across the courtyard back and forth. That's the maddest I've ever seen him. He's never laid a hand one me — ever. I've seen him really mad at other people. When he was mad at me, it was usually because he saw me doing something that was destructive to me or destructive to my career or my future. When he gets angry at me, he doesn't blow up at me. He knows how he would react if someone blew up at him and he knows that I would react the same way. When he gets mad, you don't want to be around.

"The guidance I needed, I didn't look to Dad for that, I don't think. Maybe in a lot of ways I did and was trying to take from his lifestyle without knowing it was dangerous — just putting his life into mine and ending up in trouble. In my formative years I remember worshipping the ground he walked on and thinking he was some untouchable kind of being. When I realized that he was a real person, that he was my father and he loved me and all that kind of stuff, I took a step backward and said, 'Wow! I've been torturing myself for years thinking that he was some kind of deity when, in fact, he's just papa.'"

Once MacKenzie began to emulate her father's life style her problems mounted, but regardless of her problems she would turn to John for help, as he explains. "MacKenzie used to call me all the time from different parts of the world. She'd be broke, lost her wallet, had no credit cards, homeless and wandering around.

"It always seemed like she had a charmed life. She was in *American Graffiti*. She did *One Day At A Time* and other movies and shows (*Baretta*, *Mary Tyler Moore*). What turned out to be a charmed life became tarnished for a while. We would have to pick up the pieces here and there."

In the fall of 1972 John's first single on CBC Records, *Revolution On Vacation*, was released, but it was a discouraging failure. At the same time Cass recorded two solo albums for RCA, CASS ELLIOT and THE ROAD IS NO PLACE FOR A LADY, and a year later her third album, DON'T CALL ME MAMA, was released. Cass also became a regular host on the *Tonight Show*, standing in for Johnny Carson a dozen times or so, and she had her own television show, *Don't Call Me Mama*. Denny had likewise set his sights on a solo career, recording the album WATCHA GONNA DO in 1971, while Michelle pursued her acting career after appearing in *The Last Movie* in 1970 with Dennis Hopper, whom she married but then separated from eight days later. In 1971 she had begun dating another one of the stars of *Easy Rider*, Jack Nicholson. The Mamas and The Papas had begun to live Hollywood lives.

In July 1973, John accused ABC Dunhill Records of theft from the artists who recorded for them, including himself. The case was not settled until 1985 when ABC Dunhill paid back close to half a million dollars to their artists. With his recording career in the doldrums, John and Genevieve worked up a summer cabaret act and played Reno Sweeny's in The Village. Then during July 1974, they released their first collaborative album, ROMANCE IS ON THE ROOF, which failed to capture attention, selling barely 10,000 copies.

The course of events in the lives of The Mamas and The Papas came to a crossroads on 29 July 1974 when Cass was found dead in her London hotel room, the apparent victim of choking. Former Village comedian and now talk show host Dick Cavett witnessed the profound shock that John suffered when he learned of Cass's death. "It was my friend, Marshall Brickman, who told me about this legendary character John Phillips. I didn't meet him until years later. I have an image of horseback riding once with John and Genevieve. It's a genuine image, it's not a dream. We actually went horseback riding.

"We were sitting in the house that he was renting for the summer, sort of fooling around, and I remember thinking, 'What an amusing guy he was — good company, laughing and carrying on.' Then the phone rang.

"There was this sort of long pause and he said, 'Oh my God!' then hung up the phone. 'Cass is dead.'

"I was part of that dramatic moment in his life."

John could hardly accept the fact that Cass had died. His grief was genuine. "I miss her very much. I couldn't believe it when she died. It was a closed casket funeral. Actually, her mother Beth and I couldn't believe she was in there — in the casket. I thought it was some kind of strange thing or something. She was so vibrant and so intelligent. Her mind was so roomy, she could entertain so many thoughts at the same time. I just couldn't believe she had died.

"I talked to her the night before. She had played a place called Talk of the Town, in London. She called me and said, 'Oh God, I was a great success. The reviews are wonderful.'

"The next morning it was all gone. What she really wanted was to be a success on her own. I was so proud and happy for her. She went so quickly. A day didn't pass and she was gone.

"It's funny, I didn't really have any emotion when I got the call that Cass had died. They were shipping her body back from London. It wasn't until the funeral. That's when it all hit me. I just cracked. I broke into hysterics. I pounded on the casket.

"Dying on a ham sandwich is a dumb story. It was so crazy. We investigated and found out what really happened. Actually, it's not very pretty. I saw the coroner's report and there was no ham in her at all — not in her esophagus or in her stomach. The reporter just made that story up on the spot because he didn't know what to do. It was a foreign country."

Cass's death from a coronary failure was no less traumatic for Denny. "Cass was always a fat little kid who lost her hair when she was going to grade school. Then she had scarlet fever, or some high fever, and had to put a stocking cap on when she went to school. She had to grow up with, 'Don't be seen, don't be heard, lay in the background and maybe nobody will tease or bother you or make you feel like less than you really are.'

"When she was accepted as Mama Cass she could do no wrong in her personal life, nor in her professional life. It was like she blossomed, 'Oh God! I can take my stocking cap off. No one cares if I'm three hundred pounds. If I want, I could be five hundred pounds — it doesn't matter.'

"Except her heart, dumb bitch, traveling alone. If somebody had been there, but no one was there. She was all alone, poor baby. She was just blossoming, she was coming forth."

Cass's funeral on August 2nd at Hollywood's Memorial Cemetery was a celebrity-studded affair. Her body was cremated and the ashes buried in Hebrew Cemetery, Woodlawn, Maryland.

Denny's second solo album, WAITING FOR A SONG, was released during the late summer of 1974, and he was signed as one of the stars of John and Genevieve's musical, *Space*. After countless rewrites, meetings, and arguments, rehearsals began for *Space*, an agonizing process John remembers. "Paul Morrissey, the guy who directed the musical, is now directing Hollywood movies. He had never directed a musical before, worked with dancers, or any kind of Broadway stage production. Paul is really a sweet man — we had a lot of good times together — but Paul had no sense of rhythm or dance. His musical education was right out of the book. He could turn on a classical station and, no matter what the piece was, could tell you who wrote it, in what year and all that. But he couldn't hum the melody — he couldn't carry a tune in a bucket. I've never seen Paul dance in my entire life, or make a move that wasn't sort of a little awkward.

"When we were casting the show, Paul was attracted to people like himself, who had no sense of time or music and couldn't dance — this happened to be a musical. So, we ended up with a cast of people who couldn't dance, sing, or really act."

Denny is even less flattering when he recalls what it was like to be a cast member in *Space*, which was re-named *The Man on the Moon* before opening. "I recall trying to dance on stage with Monique Van Vooren, who, I think, was clinically blind. She had detached retinas from an accident. She couldn't really see. Try dancing with a person in high heels who is blind and wants to hold onto you with a death grip.

"We rehearsed on the third floor of Andy Warhol's factory. His factory was weird. You never knew what was going to happen one day to the next. We were trying to rehearse a Broadway play with choreographers and musicians when some freak with wings, guitar, and 'lederhosen' would come dancing through.

"'Who's that?'"

"'New wave.'

"Day-to-day it was a zoo.

"John was constantly rewriting. I met my wife there; she was in the chorus. She wound up assistant director at one point. We would be in the theater rehearsing with stage hands sitting up in the grid going, 'Yeah, this is good.' They couldn't work when we were on stage. We're sitting around waiting for John to send rewrites down.

"Two weeks before we opened, after rehearsing for three or four months, we change directors. Opening night there was the old director and the new director having a punch-up in front of the creme de la creme of New York. We've got security guards keeping these two off of each other's throats. They are screaming and carrying on. The security guards kick the old guy out.

"The producer said, "I want to talk to the cast.'

"We're all sitting there.

"'I think you are all a bunch of self-indulgent ingrates.'

"'Did he just insult us? Did he just say something bad about me 'cause I'll punch him in the chest and stop his heart.' That was just one of the little things.

"If we'd stayed in previews the thing would probably still be running. But we had to open. The play was about a bomb that was going to explode on the moon, change the moon's position so that the sun would reflect and shine on the earth and give more growing time to the farm belts around the world. Production of food would go up and everything would be great on earth and on and on."

The Man on the Moon was a resounding failure and a great disappointment for John. "The show ran for about four months in previews to packed houses every night," John recalls. "I begged them to never open it. Just leave it the way it was. Who wanted the New York critics to see it? It was not meant to be a Broadway show. It was more of a farce, a comedy but not in the classical sense of Broadway theater which had very strict rules of its own. I guess *Hair* was the only thing that really broke through. Maybe *Jesus Christ Superstar*, even that had a certain format to it.

"Opening night was very strange because about three weeks before, Paul was fired by one of the major backers of the show, over Andy's protest. He resented it bitterly and was replaced by a regional director from St. Louis or somewhere, who came in and put up chase lights all around the stage and palm trees. Everything really started getting lost then. He wanted complete script changes, so I tried to quit the show, too. But I wasn't allowed to quit the show. Paul was allowed to quit the show, as a matter of fact they fired him, that's how much they allowed him to quit. He was very bitter about it.

"On opening night they hired Pinkerton Guards to surround the theater to make sure that Paul wouldn't come to the show on opening night. Paul came. He put on a fake moustache, a wig, and wore glasses. He got past the Pinkerton Guards, bought a ticket, went backstage, and promptly punched out the other director behind the curtain. This was during the overture to the show.

"Everyone in New York, everyone in the world was there. Clive Barnes was waiting to tear it to pieces — the vultures were all around us. Suddenly, about half way through the overture a palm tree comes crashing through the curtain onto the stage. The actors are trying to focus on their lines and music as this fight is going on. Bodies are being thrown. Some people thought it was part of the show. They thought it was great and were applauding.

"Denny was rather deep in his cups at the time. In his very first scene an amazing thing happened. Genevieve played the part of the littlest angel, from another planet. Denny played Vernon von Bon. Denny completely forgot his opening lines and he says, lips not moving, 'For God's sake help me' — the same thing Ed Sullivan said. I thought this was the funniest part of the whole evening.

"During intermission I just left. It was diabolical, it was just horrible. It ran that one night on Broadway! I think I hold the distinction of having garnered the worst reviews of any Broadway show ever published. It was a great disappointment.

"Clive Barnes said, 'The only bomb at the Little Theater last night was on the stage.'"

Within weeks of the show closing, Denny decided to give up show business and returned to Canada with his then girlfriend Jeanette, where he picked up work acting for Neptune Theatre and then hosted his own music variety show. With Mama Cass dead, there was little left of The Mamas and The Papas except bittersweet memories. They may have set out in the 1970s to make their own kind of music, but by mid-decade there was no music coming from any of the Mamas or the Papas.

John Phillips (opposite) and Michelle with their daughter Chynna Phillips, who would form the band Wilson Phillips with Brian Wilson's daughters a generation later. John's daughters MacKenzie Phillips and Bijou Phillips would also pursue recording and acting careers. (Photos by Guy Webster)

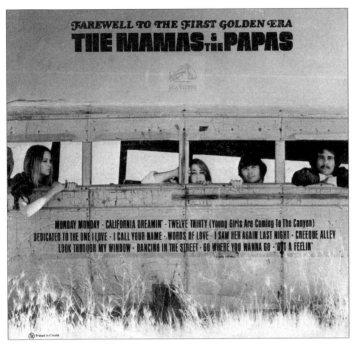

The Mamas and
The Papas said
farewell to their
fans on their
"Golden Era"
greatest hits album
but returned to
record "People
Like Us."
(Album photos by
Guy Webster, top,
and Henry Diltz,
bottom)

THE MAMAS
THE PAPAS

TRIP, STUMBLE
AND FALL

Trip, Stumble and Fall

You're goin' to trip, stumble and fall
And though I know you're havin' a ball
You'd better listen my friend
This is the end
Someone's goin' to make you cry
You're goin' to trip, stumble and fall . . .

(John Phillips, ASCAP)

I f the late 1960s were years of great achievement for The Mamas and
The Papas, the late 1970s, although holding as much promise, were
years of great disappointment. John worked with Nick Roge on the
film *The Man Who Fell To Earth* and began recording a new album with
Mick Jagger and Keith Richards. Denny took to the amateur stage in
Halifax, acting in plays produced at the Neptune Theatre, before host-
ing a television music variety show, which Michelle and John graced
with an appearance. Michelle recorded her first solo album, VICTIM OF
ROMANCE, then co-starred with Rudolph Nureyev in the film *Valentino*.
But by the end of the decade, John had descended into an abyss of drug

addictions, Denny had succumbed to alcoholism, and Michelle found herself performing in Brazil.

During 1975, David Bowie recommended John Phillips to write the score for the Nick Roge film *The Man Who Fell to Earth*, an opportunity John welcomed with confidence, despite the problems he faced with his work in musicals. "Nick Roge, an Englishman and a very fine film director, called me and said that he had this movie that he had completed all shooting on," John recalls. "They hadn't finished the editing. It starred Candy Clark (an American actress) and David Bowie. David had done a sound track for the movie and the producers just didn't like it. They had asked David, 'Who would you like to do it, because we don't like what you've done with it? We'd like to give you the opportunity to choose someone else.'

"'Why don't you have John Phillips do it?'

"Nick and I had known each other for years and that was fine with Nick. Nick called and said, 'If you're interested, I'll come over to the States and show you the film without any music, just dialogue.'

"So, he came over and we went to Candy Clark's house. He had a video cassette of the film. I thought the film was fabulous, just really great — I love it. I told him that afternoon that 'I'd be glad to do it, more than an honor to do it.'

"Three days later I was in London. As soon as I got to London, I went to the music department of British Lion. I said, 'Just out of interest I'd like to hear the score that David had written for the show just so I could see what they didn't like.' They played the score and it was fabulous. It was so good — it was really good. All full of wind chimes and Japanese instruments. It just fit the mood of the movie perfectly. I couldn't understand, for the life of me, why they wanted somebody else to do it when they had this beautiful, beautiful score. I've always wondered what David did with that? I guess a lot of that ended up in part of his future albums since then.

"I went back to Nick and said, 'Nick what's going on? This score is great. It fits the film so beautifully and David did such a great job. He worked forever getting it done.'

"'Yeah, I know but they have the money, and they're producing the show. They don't like it. They want it to be more American with banjos and folk guitars — more of an American feel.'

"In the story a spaceman lands in America but it has an oriental sort of flavor to it all the time, which David carries about him in some strange fashion. I'm not sure how he carries it off, but he does.

"'I just don't understand it.'

"'I don't either, to tell you the truth.'

"So, I went ahead and did it. David does all the acting in the film, and I do all the singing. I used Mick Taylor on guitar and some of the English musicians for the studio dates. I think Keith Richards played on a couple of things. We all became very fast friends. Fast friends is a good term as a matter of fact — very close friends. Keith and I and Mick Jagger would hang out a lot together, and Mick Taylor also.

"Keith had a son named Marlon who was the same age as my son Tamerlane. I guess they were seven or eight years old at the time. We would sit around, play guitar, and do coke all night. We'd sing old Everly Brothers songs and that kind of stuff."

John's relationship with members of The Rolling Stones grew closer over those months in England working on *The Man Who Fell To Earth*, to the extent that he planned to record his next album in collaboration with Jagger, Richards, and Taylor, as John explains. "I sang a whole group of songs for Mick (Jagger) that I had written since '71 up until '75 but hadn't published or recorded.

"'Gee, these are great songs. You've got to do them,' Mick said.

"'I don't really have any motivation to do them right now,' I replied. 'I just finished *Man Who Fell To Earth* and the Broadway show, which was a complete flop. I'll just take it easy for a while.'

"I was getting into heroin, at that time, and that sort of made me a little on the lazy side.

"'Well I tell you what. I'll produce the album if you'll be the artist and do the songs.'

"Mick got Keith Richards involved and we started doing it. It was sort of a funny project because Mick finally realized that Keith and I were so loaded that he was just going to drop out of it and sort of stop the violence for a while. Keith and I would take like five or six hours to tune our guitars before we could even start cutting the tracks. The engineers are sitting around and the other musicians are sitting around.

"'Oh! I have to go to the bathroom. I'll be right back.' We'd show up an hour later, that kind of thing."

Recording engineer Harvey Goldberg noticed a big change in John from the first time he had met him. Working in the studio with John and Keith became a depressing experience because of their drug abuse. "I first met John, I believe it was either 1972 or 1973," Goldberg recalls. "I must have been about nineteen at the time. Of course, I had heard of The Mamas and The Papas. I'd always been a fan. When I first met John he was definitely somebody you could tell who had just come off the hippie scene of the late '60s. He was one of the biggest stars out of that whole scene.

"When I ran into him again, he was working with The Stones. There was a big difference the way he looked physically. He had lost a lot of weight and did not look healthy. I wasn't really sure what was wrong because I had never really seen anything like that before. He was a lot more withdrawn, where before he was very outgoing, quite an extrovert, always cracking jokes. He always had something to say. There was definitely a difference, both physically and personality wise.

"When I started to work on the record I was very excited about it because, first of all, I think John's a great writer. He was doing a collaboration with The Stones, which is a band that I think is terrific. I thought it was going to be a pretty exciting project to do. Within two sessions I found we weren't really getting that much done.

"There was an entourage that was always around the sessions, more than was supposed to be at the sessions. When John would arrive, he'd be pretty well out of it. Because of the hours they were working, a lot of times we wouldn't finish until daybreak, and it pretty well kept me out of touch with the rest of the world. I found myself surrounded by people that I really didn't want to be around.

"The sessions, in general, were pretty funny because it was the type of thing where they wouldn't always show up for the sessions or they'd show up easily two to three hours late. When we were starting the session the day that Elvis died, I was wondering if maybe everybody was actually going to take a break. But, sure enough, about one or two in the morning everybody came wandering into the studio. There were a couple jokes about Elvis's death because the people, such as John, who were coming in on the session were pretty much involved in the drug scene themselves and they seemed aware of the fact that Elvis had been involved with drugs — they were junkies making fun of other junkies.

"We were supposed to start around nine in the evening. Quite often I'd get a call around midnight saying that they would be there in about an hour. They were just waiting for somebody to show up. Then I'd get a call an hour later from them saying that they'd be there in twenty minutes. They would either show up a good three to four hours late or I'd finally get a call that they weren't going to make it in that night. I found it very depressing.

"Going back to the entourage that used to be around, a lot of these people were drug dealers and friends. There was a girl whose husband or boyfriend was a drug supplier and she was hanging around the session. I was waiting for everybody to show up and she started talking to me. She asked me if I wanted to see her scrap book.

"'Yeah sure.'

"So she pulls out this scrap book. I expected it to be photographs of people she met, or whatever. Instead, it was prescriptions for drugs throughout the past few centuries — I mean dating back to the 1600s and 1700s.

"I thought, 'mmmmmmmmmm, pretty strange.'

"A lot of the melodies to the songs were very strong. John's always been pretty good with words because he's quite a bright guy. He has a good command of the English language. There was a difference between what he was writing during that period and what he was writing in the '60s. During the '60s he was writing about personal experiences. During that period he was writing about what was happening to him in the drug scene. I don't think anybody — other than junkies — could relate to the lyrics.

"I remember having a talk with John at one point, trying to make him aware that this was the direction the songs were going and that he had very strong songs if he could start to write lyrics that could appeal on a mass level so that the people could relate to them. I told him that, if he did, he would probably have a very strong album. He was so out of touch at that point I don't think what I said meant anything to him.

"Mick and John had been friends a long time. They obviously went back a long way. I got the feeling that Mick got involved because they were friends and I think he was almost trying to give John something to do because he was hoping that it might straighten him out. It was a combination of somebody trying to help him out, but, at the same time, being tolerant of what he was going through because, obviously, he'd seen a lot of that around him also.

"During the period that Keith was having all those drug problems in Toronto, I believe he was getting ready to start straightening himself out. This episode was probably like one sort of last binge, or something that he was enjoying with John. The two of them looked like pretty run-down characters.

"We used to finish in the studio somewhere around daybreak and they were outside the studio. I guess they were waiting for me to come out. One of the secretaries at the studio was arriving for work. New York has a lot of street bums and, from a distance, as she was walking to the studio, she was thinking, 'of all the places they have to pick to stand in front of, why do they have to pick the studio?' As she got closer she realized that it was in fact John Phillips and Keith Richards.

"The sessions just deteriorated to nothing. Whereas we used to get something done, maybe, every three days, which for me felt like way behind schedule, it was now to the point that nothing was getting done. Finally it just dwindled to a stop. John disappeared and I believe the next time I heard about him was the bust."

In a word, John had become a junkie, as he recognized years later, though he still tried to pass himself off as capable of handling his addiction. "No other people around me, especially Jagger, realized how deeply I was in," John recalls. "Mick is the master of understatement. I was in the kitchen cooking a spoon of heroin over the burner. Mick came in.

"'Don't you think you're getting a little deep into this?'

"'No, I can handle it.'

"'Oh man, I've heard people say that before.'

"He turned and walked out. That was his only sort of chastisement the whole time. The rest of the time he was a very helpful — trying to help things along to get me through all this. Mick has his tight rope act down perfectly. He can balance himself no matter where he is. He has an equilibrium on both sides of the pendulum. He's able to walk back and forth. I'm not that way.

"Mick once said he had just done something outrageous at a club or something.

"'How can you do that kind of stuff?'

"'I'm a bit more bombastic than you are, John.'

"It turned out he was right in certain instances and other ones he was wrong. I was sort of a no turn-around guy. I was a commitment kind of person. Once I got into drugs it took me a long time to really find my way back out again."

Phillips, Jagger, and Richards were nevertheless able to complete thirteen tracks for the album, though their creative collaboration ended in a dispute over ownership of the publishing rights for the songs, "not among Mick, Keith, me, but between Atlantic Records and myself," John explains. "I got the rights back to the album later. We've been calling it 'The Lost Album' for years and years. It has some of the best performances by Keith on guitar and vocals by Mick. We did trios together and we did duets. I did a lot of solo stuff and Michelle sang on it. Mick Taylor plays guitar. Charlie Watts and Ron Wood are also on it. It's a great album." Rumor has it that this 'lost' album has been found and may be released.

During the first nine months of 1976, John and Genevieve Phillips traveled extensively, first in South Africa, followed by two weeks in Venezuela for a brief holiday in April, then to England in June. Without telling Michelle, they booked passage on the *Queen Elizabeth II* — to surprise her. Michelle was on her way to London to star with Rudolph Nureyev in the movie *Valentino*.

While in England, John teamed up with Keith Richards again to celebrate Christmas. Richards owned a medieval castle in the English countryside, and he invited John and his family to celebrate the Christmas season (1976) with his family. John was delighted to accept. "I had my mom come over from the States. She was in her seventies. MacKenzie had the *One Day at a Time* show going very well for her so I invited her to come as well. We all went to a place called Redlands, a house built in the 17th century that Keith owns about an hour outside of London. Mom, whose Indian name is Buffalo Eyes, had assimilated beautifully into American society. She had pink hair, a house in the valley with a swimming pool, and a Lincoln. She was in heaven. And here she was at one of The Rolling Stones' homes for Christmas. She just couldn't believe the whole thing was happening.

"Keith and I would go upstairs and do some drugs. We'd come downstairs and we'd be a little shaky. Mom would turn to MacKenzie and say, 'He looks like the pictures. He's on drugs, isn't he?'

"'Oh no, Grandma. He's not on drugs.'

"Keith and I would be knocking everything over.

"Genevieve was there the whole time, as were Anita, Tamerlane, and Marlon. It was a wild Christmas. We bought the kids electric automobiles. They would be racing up and down stairs, all over the place. Chynna was also there.

"They had a burglar alarm system which was activated by pushing a button. It rang in the local police station. There was a button in the children's room. Anita went to great pains to explain to Tamerlane that if you push this button, the police will come and chase the robbers away. Tam sort of interpreted it as meaning before you go to bed push the button and no robbers will come. So, at about nine or ten o'clock, the kids are getting trundled off to bed and the last thing Tam does is push the button. We were all smoking grass in the living room and talking — there are drugs all over the house.

"Genevieve is sitting on the couch — they had a big picture window. 'I could swear I see balloons bouncing across the picture window.'

"I look up, 'Balloons?'

"'Yeah, there's five of them bouncing up and down.'

"'Balloons! Those are Bobbies' hats. It was the English police answering the alarm. Toilets started flushing all over the house. We successfully talked our way out of it.

"There had already been a lot of publicity about Keith being on drugs and me being on drugs. Most of it was true. We were living together in the same house in London for about four or five months before Keith and Anita Pallenberg and Marlon, their son, found their own house, which happened to be about three blocks away on one side and Mick three blocks on the other side. It was quite a time around that area."

Former Kingston Trio member John Stewart, songwriter of The Monkee's hit Daydream Believer, and one of John's old friends, has a special perspective on John Phillips' addiction to drugs — and to The Rolling Stones. "I knew he was doing this album with Mick Jagger.

John always flaunted the most outrageous aspects of himself. The friends that I knew, who knew Jagger, would say that this guy could really turn you on. He was in a real dangerous atmosphere. John was not only able to hang on with this crowd and be on equal terms, he could be in control a lot of times.

"It was an amazing thing, his ability to talk people into doing things and his ability to stay on top of a situation — to throw up smoke and mirrors and get what he wanted it was remarkable. He would have been a brilliant attorney."

When John and Genevieve returned to New York in February 1977, his sister Rosie was shocked by John's state of health. She was sure he was about to die, as she recalls. "When I first realized the depth that he was into drugs, I was traveling a lot with MacKenzie, as her guardian. We always ended up in New York — or somewhere — where we could spend some time with John before we went back to California. We were staying at a hotel, being paid for by Warner Brothers, so we were having a big time. I went to see John. He weighed about 130 pounds. He looked like he belonged in a casket. All I could see were bones, hollow stomach, every bone outlined and needle marks all over him and ulcerated places.

"I was so shocked because I knew he was using drugs, but I hadn't seen him. I had no idea that he had reached that point — that was one of the lowest points. He had been in the hospital and he had been shooting up in his foot. It had become very infected and they almost had to amputate his foot. At the last minute he responded to the antibiotics. He had just come from that and that's when I saw him.

"Again, there goes the tears. I started crying 'cause I thought he was going to die. I didn't believe I would ever see him again. He continued to use drugs but pulled himself out of that hole where he was using just pure heroin and then he started the cocaine trip. To me that was the saddest moment."

Fearful about her father's drug addiction, MacKenzie turned to Mick Jagger for help. "I was about eighteen. I was living with Peter Asher, a record producer We lived at the Chateau Elmont in Hollywood. Dad was in New York. I thought he was going to die on me — I was so frightened. I was into drugs but I wasn't into needles. That hadn't come into play yet. I was just scared for Dad.

"I knew Mick Jagger was in town. I called him and he came over to our suite at the Chateau Elmont. I took him into the bedroom.

"'Mick, we've got to do something. What can we do?

"'I can't stop your father, you can't stop your father.'

"'He may not be here tomorrow.'

"We just sat there and I remember we both wept. I was trying to reach out. I didn't know who to reach out to 'cause I couldn't get in touch with Dad. Everywhere I called it was, 'Oh, he just left' — he was avoiding me."

John's drug abuse may not have killed him but drugs led to his arrest and imprisonment. John talks candidly about how he got involved with Sidney Korn and Alvin Broad in drug trafficking at their K&B Drugs at 81st and Madison in downtown New York in July of 1977. "I had been doing drugs in England. This was after I came back from England. I was staying at a hotel across from the Metropolitan Museum in New York. The drug store was right around the corner. I walked in to get some toiletries. MacKenzie was with me.

"Keith and a bunch of people were in New York and there was a real shortage of syringes. Not like these days where you can go down to the beach and pick them up. We were very fastidious in our drug habits about keeping everything really clean to avoid disease and things like that. We knew that much, anyway. A lot of people didn't realize that much. We had no education about drugs. We just knew you got high for a while, then you took some more and got high again. When that wore off, you took some more and you got high again — that was it.

"I bought some toothpaste, talc, a razor, and saw a box of syringes up on the shelf. I said to the pharmacist, almost kiddingly, 'Oh, I'd like a box of those, too.'

"'Okay, we'll send them over to you later. What hotel are you staying at?' About an hour later a guy knocked at the door and delivered all my toiletries and a box of a hundred syringes.

"To a person who was addicted to intravenous drug use, it was like heaven. You couldn't imagine the find — 'clean works', as they call them on the streets. It was almost impossible. In fact, you couldn't really tell if they were clean or not.

"I don't think that they meant any harm. They just realized that I was sort of in desperate straits, and I think they thought that they were being helpful to themselves and to me at the same time. It was like a trade off situation. It wasn't as though I was a helpless junkie walking in and they were taking advantage of me. I knew perfectly well what I was getting myself into. Not being a 'turn back kind of person', I was ready to jump right in.

"The next day I went over and talked to them some more and got some more things. After about a month had gone by, we were very close friends as well as business associates. I guess over a period of — oh — three, four years, I must have taken ten thousand Quaaludes out of that place. I'd go in, or Keith would go in, but it was mostly me. Bill Cleary went once and said I was completely insane.

"I'd go in with a shopping bag and a list. We'd go down the list and we'd fill the bag with a thousand Quaaludes, this many Nembutals, this many Tuinals, things that required triplicates (prescription forms). We would buy the triplicates from thieves who would hit doctor's offices at night. They would rob the New York triplicate prescription pads and sell them on the streets for like two hundred bucks for a pad of one hundred triplicate prescriptions. I would give them to the druggist and they would put phony names on them, like tombstone names, and dispense the drugs to me."

Bill Cleary saw first-hand how John and K&B Drugs operated their illegal drug scheme. "John had mentioned this drugstore, but I thought it was a drugstore where he had a doctor that was writing him 'scripts. He was getting into it heavily. He would go to the drugstore with the 'scripts and get whatever he needed. I didn't know the 'scripts were coming from another source and that it was totally illegal. The pharmacist would actually fill out the doctor's name and give him anything he wanted. It looked kind of right when he walked in and he'd give him a triplicate book, you'd think a doctor gave it to him and he'd get everything he wanted."

One day John asked Bill Cleary to help him count the prescriptions. "'That's a pretty good deal. You got a doctor writing all those?' He gave me a book of triplicates.

"'Count the 'scripts in that book for me.' I counted the 'scripts. There's no signatures, no doctor's signature, or no quantity of drug. These guys at K&B would just fill out the whole thing. As long as you had the books, they could get covered. They used to deal with a lot of hospitals so they had quite a volume of drugs. I found that out and I kept telling him to stop. He was just back in the same ol' situation.

"I talked to him in the kitchen and said, 'John, I can't help you and you are not helping yourself. You've broken every federal law that has to do with DEA or narcotics. We're talking about a hundred years here if someone is caught on this. I think it's going to come down very quickly.'"

During this period, Hollywood casting director Michael McLean visited John in New York. "While I was in New York, I called John and went to see him. It wasn't John — it was a drug dependent. I had seen intravenous drug users over the years. It became obvious to me that John was using smack or some drug intravenously. I sat John down. 'Hey man, this isn't you. This isn't John Phillips. What are you into here? What's happening to you?' With his usual charm John would talk around it and through it. He denied that there was a problem. I was very concerned about him because I cared a lot for John. It was a different person, it wasn't him.

"It wasn't long after that John and Genevieve showed up in Hollywood, and asked to stay in my home. They had some sort of electronic equipment that Keith Richards had given them. I don't know exactly how it worked, but whenever they wanted a fix they were supposed to push a button and it would give them a shock. They were in terrible shape. After they had been at my house for a few days, I said, this is insanity. I can't live with this. I took them to the Le Parc Hotel and checked them in. They had no money so, of course, I had to put it on my credit card. I don't think I ever got stuck with the bill. I don't know how we got around that. I think John ended up taking care of it or maybe his attorney, at that time, became responsible for it. John and Genevieve were literally bouncing off the wall. I would get distraught phone calls from the manager of the hotel.

"'You've got to get these people out of here.'

"'I'm not looking after them. I'll come over and talk to them, but you're going to have to deal with them directly.'"

Bill Cleary witnessed the deceit and physical deterioration which ensued. "John began using make-up on his hands to hide the marks. It worked really well, but his vision wasn't that great and it was obvious that this guy was putting make-up all over his body — any place that had a mark. He'd just slap it on, rub it on, and it would cover. We're not talking about someone who doesn't know anything about cosmetics. When asked about the make-up, his reply was, 'I just got off a show.'

"'Well, smooth it down a little more. It's caked around your eyes.' It was always caked somewhere. He had big globs of it here and there."

As a favor to Denny, John and Michelle agreed to reunite for an appearance on his TV show in Halifax in early 1978. Michelle was not prepared for what happened, as she explains. "I have a copy of that tape and I've never been able to bring myself to even look at it.

"We did it because Denny had a show and Denny wanted us. I was happy to do it. At this point I knew about John's addiction. I had also been told by John that it was all under control, we should go to Halifax and do it — we'd be great and that would be that. I made John swear to me that even though he was saying that he was clean, he certainly wouldn't take any drugs across the (Canadian) border.

"'Oh, don't worry. I'll never do anything like that.'

"When we got to Halifax, it was apparent that he was doing drugs and running out of them, which was even worse — it was horrible. John was gray and sick. I had never seen John in this condition. It was a particularly frightening thing for me to see first-hand.

"John had moved to New York by that point, and I hadn't seen him in a year, or at least several months. The physical deterioration was so frightening. It made it almost impossible to do the show. All I wanted to do was get out of there."

Like the good friend he is, Bill Cleary tried to help. "I had a place at Newport Beach, right across from Delbow Island. It was real nice 'cause all the boats came in. It had five bedrooms, a dock at the end of the house, a nice walkway and a telephone on the dock. John and Genevieve came to visit me there.

"John fell out of the limo. Genevieve is stumbling. They were both in bad shape. They stayed . . . I don't know how long. I told them I didn't want any drugs in the house. I used to make them ride a bicycle and take them on walks. We would walk up and down the board walk. We'd walk, go to lunch, eat the right foods — a lot of fruit."

With Bill's help, John and Genevieve did recover long enough to take Tamerlane back, but John soon resumed his drug abuse. He happened to find a doctor who would prescribe some drugs for him.

"Once a person gets cleaned up and realizes they've cleaned up, they figure, 'Okay, I can handle this now. I've cleaned up once. If I go back — I can beat this,' John comments. "You can't beat it."

John and Genevieve rented a house on Long Island Sound along Shore Road in Connecticut. Former Washington Redskin football player Steve Thurlow was surprised when he heard a rock star was moving next door. Steve remembers when the real estate agent came to see him and his wife Chris. "The realtor was a good friend of ours and came over to us and said, 'There's a rock star moving in next door. They're coming over to look at the place in another hour.' She mentioned the name, John Phillips.

"'Gee, John Phillips. I know John from Washington. Are you sure this is the same one, the one with The Mamas and The Papas?'

"'Yes.'

"I looked out the window and there was John standing on the sea wall. I remember it was just one evening that we were together in Washington. During that period I was with the Washington Redskins. Another interesting thing was the fellow who introduced my wife to me was also the fellow that introduced me to John and Bill Cleary. We were in Washington, at a restaurant and John introduced us. We sat around one night, had a few drinks, and talked about different things.

"So, here it was, how many years later, I guess about twenty, and all of a sudden this guy is moving into the house next door. I was kind of enthusiastic about it. I thought it was great. I went over and introduced myself. Sure enough, he remembers that we had met and remembered about the Redskins. He was a big sports fan.

"We didn't know the story behind what was happening. We spent quite a bit of time together. Chris spent a lot of time with Genevieve. She was really in need of emotional support and that type of thing. Over the period I doubt that there was a day that she didn't spend a couple of hours over in our house talking to Chris about different things.

"John, of course, had a definite program. We didn't know what he was doing. Late in the afternoon a limo would pull up and he would go into town.

"Two or three times a season, we'd get together and watch the Monday night ball game on TV. When the basketball season started, we watched a few. He loved basketball. He was tall and had played basketball. We talked an awful lot. We'd sit around. John and Genevieve came over and sang. Chris would sing with them. We were the only friends they had in this area."

In May 1978 John and Susie's son Jeffrey was arrested for break and entry into a Los Angeles drug store. He was looking for drugs. Later that month, Genevieve flew to Los Angeles to visit Tamerlane, and Rosie advised her to leave John. Soon after, an acrimonious custody battle for Tamerlane began between Michelle and John, as she recalls. "We had another conflict which involved Tamerlane. Tamerlane was living with me for two years during the period that John and Genevieve said they were trying to clean themselves up. When I brought Tamerlane out to California, he was in terrible emotional shape and was seeing a psychiatrist. He was doing really well. In the two years that I had him, he had made incredible strides and was a very happy little boy with a lot of insecurities. He was a completely changed kid from the time that I had him for the first time.

"Then John and Genevieve came out to California and told me that they wanted to see Tam, which I let them do (November 11, 1979). They told me that they wanted him to come and spend a night with them, which I didn't want him to do. I was afraid to let Tam go with them. It was obvious to me that, as much as they denied it, something was still going on. I didn't know the extent of it at that point, but I knew they weren't cleaned up.

"I asked them to come in and speak to Tam's psychiatrist. 'I am afraid that you're going to try to take him,' I said to John in the middle of the session with the psychiatrist. John looked at me. 'I don't know why you would think that, Michelle. You've done so much for him. I mean, I will never forget what you've done for Tamerlane and what you've done for me. Why do you think that I would take him knowing how much harm it would do to him?' Hearing John say that, I thought, well, I've really got to let him go spend the night with him. The next day Tam was gone!

"I didn't see Tamerlane again until about two months later when the police called me from Connecticut and said they had found him. John and Genevieve had been accused of child stealing. Tamerlane was in my custody. Rosemary, John's sister, had joint custody.

"This was a very serious charge, a felony, child stealing. So, when the police found the child, they called me and said, 'Come and get him. We have him in protective custody.' I was on the next plane with Rosemary. I went back East to pick him up. When we got there John had managed to get out of jail and get a local judge to put a restraining order on us so we couldn't take Tamerlane back to California. This was a test case in Connecticut of the Uniform Child Custody Act. It is a law that states if one state has already made a claim on child residency, the other state cannot ignore it. If the state has adopted it, which Connecticut just had, they act on it.

"John and Genevieve went to the hearing where they told the judge that, 'Yes, they had a drug problem once, but it was now over and they hadn't touched drugs in several months.' Genevieve was pregnant and all they were trying to do was get their family back together again.

"I lost the case and I realize that there was only so much that I could do to help Tamerlane. When Rosemary and I lost that hearing, we came back to California. I said, 'Well, all we can do is pray for this kid and let the chips fall where they may.'"

The custody battle was equally stressful for Rosie. "When Tamerlane first came to live in California, John and Genevieve let Michelle take him and signed over a witness paper giving Michelle rights to care for the boy — to call a doctor if it was necessary, make decisions about education, and this type of thing. It wasn't actually a paper saying, 'We're giving this child to Michelle.'

"When Michelle got to New York to pick him up, he was about five years old. The apartment was an utter mess. The child was filthy. All of his clothes were filthy. John and Genevieve had bought him a puppy and no one had ever cleaned up any mess. Michelle said, 'It was almost impossible to believe.' I have had the same description given to me by lots of people. A man I knew, Jim Poe, he was a writer, called me one time from John's apartment.

"'How are things?'

"'I wouldn't walk barefoot on the rugs.'

"'What do you mean?'

"'You might get stuck on something.' You know, a needle but not saying, a needle.

"Michelle brought the boy back and got him in school. He

was almost six years old, but he hadn't been to school yet. He didn't even know his ABC's. He knew nothing except what show was going to be on a particular television channel. He memorized and could recite when *Life With Father* or *Car 54* would be on. That's what he did. He watched television all day long or called room service. They lived in hotels.

"I did the grandmothering kind of role, even though I was his aunt. He was the same age as my grandson. He became very happy. Within about six months he had completely caught up with the kids of his age. He was reading, he was writing, he was doing arithmetic, and when John and Genevieve took him away, he had just been made president of his class, in third grade.

"They kidnapped him! The Superior Court, in Los Angeles, made me his legal guardian until such time that John and Genevieve could prove they were able to care for him. This was done because Genevieve kept saying, 'I'm on my way. I'm coming. I'm going to take Tam back.' There has been no improvement; if anything he's gone down hill.

"Michelle and I finally found them in Greenwich, Connecticut. I got a call from the welfare people, telling me to come and pick him up. Michelle and I flew to Connecticut. In the meantime, John had got some sort of court order. It was the strangest, unreal thing. The court order gave him temporary custody because the courts in Connecticut didn't like the way the courts in California did law. They gave temporary custody (to John and Genevieve). The permanent custody I had been given was not recognized.

"John came into court dressed like a country gentleman. He had on beautiful leather boots and a big sweater. He was very thin but he had bulky clothes on, very expensive tweeds. He made affidavits — total lies! Michelle and I tried to tell the lawyer who was defending us that this was just absolutely untrue. John was a drug dealer, that's how he was making his money — they just didn't believe us. Here was an ex-wife and older sister. They thought that we had a grudge and that we were just trying to show John that he couldn't push us around, or something like that.

"On December 21, 1979, the judge said 'No.' The child would stay with John and Genevieve until a full custody hearing could be done. We decided to just back off. We asked John if we could see Tamerlane and he finally said, 'Yes.' We went over that evening. It was around Christmas. Tam, who had been my little boy, would always want to sit on my lap, wanting me to hold him, wanting me to touch him, do things with him, suddenly wouldn't even let me touch him. Only a month had gone by. He was hiding in the basement. He had built a fortress in the basement and he was hiding. John went down and brought him up. He was holding onto John's leg, with both of his legs just wrapped around John. I went over and got near him. He started screaming. I just couldn't understand it. It was like an arrow through my heart.

"Standing in the darkened dining room was a huge, mob-looking guy. John had connections. I guess this guy was a bodyguard he had hired to protect his wife and child from Michelle and me. The whole thing was like it wasn't real — it wasn't happening. We finally left with total dissatisfaction.

"Michelle grabbed the wreath off the front door, threw it in the driveway, and drove her car back and forth, back and forth, on it while they all stood at the windows watching. I kept saying, 'Don't do this Michelle! Don't do this! It's Christmas.' But she did."

Because Tamerlane was like a son to Bill Cleary, he became an unwitting partner to a ruse to help prove to the authorities that John was drug clean, a condition for gaining custody of Tam, as Cleary explains. "It had to do with getting Tam back. John had to stay clean. He needed someone with clean urine because his urine was not clean — he was doing drugs. I wouldn't have done it but Tam was like a son to me. I spent a lot of time on the road with him. He's a great friend. I'd do anything to help Tam.

"We get some of those plastic lemons and wash them. I urinated into the lemons. John buys some jockey shorts and plans to put the lemon into the jockey shorts. If it's an unsupervised urinalysis, they may be standing outside and no one is watching, they hear you going into the bottle. That's it!

"I did two lemons. I put one in the freezer and the other one I had was warm, so John was ready to go. I threw him the one that had been in the freezer. He did a double take — I mean, it's frozen solid.

"'How am I going to use this? What good is this to me?'

"We have frozen urine!"

About this time, Chris and Steve Thurlow discovered proof of John and Genevieve's drug usage in a perplexing way, as Chris recounts. "One day I came back from grocery shopping and, as I got out of the car in the driveway, I noticed that there was water coming out of a sewage vent on the outside of John's house. I walked over to it and there were probably twenty-five or thirty blue-and-white hypodermic needles, syringes, coming out of the side of the house. I was rather perplexed and tried to be sort of casual about it. Just as I was walking back into the house, John drove in, in his little white Mustang. I walked over and, in a rather accusatory way, I said, 'John why are there hypodermic needles coming out of your house?'

"He looked down, 'There's a very good explanation and I'll tell you in a few minutes.' I went into my house and started to put my groceries away. John came over and he had a little vial with him.

"'I have been giving Genevieve vitamin shots, she's very anaemic.'

"'Who asked you to give them to her? Why would someone allow you?'

"'Genevieve's doctor asked me to do this.'

"What doctor, her gynaecologist? Who is this man? If he's somebody here in town, he ought to have his licence taken away.'

"'I'll find out.' John ran home.

"He came back.

'Did I say Genevieve?'

"'Yes.'

"'I meant Trelawny, the dog.'

"'Trelawny's gynaecologist has asked you to give your dog shots?'

"'Did I say gynaecologist? I meant veterinarian.'

"'What for?'

"'Trelawny has mange.'

"'Why aren't you disposing of the needles?'

"He explained that because of the custody battle he was concerned that Michelle may have spies going through his garbage and trash. With his past history of drugs, this could lead to having Tamerlane taken away. He was looking for a safe means of disposal and decided to flush them down the john.

"In the year subsequent to John having lived there, every time a new bush was planted or wallpaper is taken down from the attic, there were a hundred more needles that come cascading forward. Obviously, there was a very large quantity being used.

"I said to my husband, I know John said to you that he wasn't doing any drugs, but, obviously, there is something going on over there. There are all of these syringes pouring out of the house. At which point, my husband gave me the 'don't be such a pessimist' lecture. I should give everybody the benefit of the doubt. That was probably the first half-a-dozen incidents that built up to the point where we knew."

Steve Thurlow was more willing to take what John said at face value than his wife. "Chris is always much more suspect of people than I am. I'm always willing to take two-and-a-half strikes before I'm ready to strike somebody out. So, I kept believing John because he was always so conscientious about coming up with the right answer, at the right time. The guy is so sharp. He could make you a believer. He always seemed to have some kind of response that made some sense. We went along, even though we saw these five or six incidents that indicated to us something was going on.

"I, more or less, assumed that he was telling us the truth. If he wasn't, it probably wasn't that big a deal that there was some little, lingering thing that was still going on in their lives, as far as drugs were concerned.

"It was Katie's (the Thurlow's daughter) first communion dinner. We invited John, Gen, MacKenzie, and Tam to have dinner with us. We went to church in the morning and stayed dressed. It was like Easter Sunday. They were supposed to be here at 7:30. John came over about 8:30 and the rest of them came over about 9:15. John went back and forth. It was one of those deals where it was a constant back and forth (between houses). 'I've got to take some antihistamines. I have to check the phone' — back and forth. The dinner was going to start at 8 o'clock. It turned out that we didn't sit down until 10.

"In the meantime I was sitting in the living room and John and Gen were there. At one point Gen and I were having a conversation and John went to the telephone. I think he felt he was far enough away from me that I couldn't hear. He had called someone and you could tell that there was a lot of nervousness going on. Something was happening. I wasn't sure what it was. John called someone who we later traced back afterwards. We became suspicious of the whole situation.

We found out that it was the person who was selling some of the drugs and pills to him from Poughkeepsie, New York.

John said, 'Listen, we'd really like to see you later tonight. We're all anxious to see you. What time can you get over here?' He said this about four times. I'm thinking, I thought we were having dinner. I didn't know what time of night he's talking about but we were going to have dinner.

"'Just bring over the same things that you brought the other day.' I'm thinking, they're not talking about pyjamas. There is something going on. Somebody's bringing something over that has to be there that night. I was very suspicious at that point and, of course, dinner was very strange — it was a weird dinner.

"They were not in good shape, and later that evening after they had left, we realized that John's raincoat had been left in our closet. We took it out. Inside the pockets were quite a few syringes plus a big booklet of maybe two hundred prescriptions that were made out to some doctor from New York, and a tourniquet — so very suspicious. 'Hey, that's it!' This is what we heard. The things that we found in his coat and the fact that Chris had been very suspicious guaranteed that there was definitely something going on. I guess it was at this point that we realized that all of the innocence they had portrayed, protesting that there were no drugs in the family, was definitely not true."

Chris tells a harrowing tale of her discovery of the extent of John and Genevieve's drug abuse. "John and Gen went away for a week and left the dog in the house. The dog was howling and carrying on. I was very concerned about it. I called the owners of the house in New Jersey and asked permission to go in and get the dog out. My sister, Hillary, who is a physician, and at that time medical officer with the Suffix County Prison, and I took a ladder and climbed into the house through an upstairs window.

"What we found was absolutely phenomenal. I had never been allowed upstairs. The downstairs was filthy, but it was nothing like what the upstairs was. There were needles lying around. There were candy wrappers. Cigarette butts had been put out in every manner of furniture including the sheets and on the rug. The bed had collapsed and the mattress was lying in the middle of the collapsed bed. In the bathroom were charred spoons."

On 31 March 1980, Genevieve gave birth to their daughter on the couch of their Connecticut home while John was stoned out of his mind and MacKenzie was asleep upstairs. In an effort to break their addiction, which proved futile, John and MacKenzie checked into a rehab center in New Canaan, Connecticut. Soon after their discharge, Genevieve was admitted to a hospital in Milford, Connecticut after suffering from violent seizures coming off barbiturates. In July Mick Jagger and Jerry Hall paid a visit and were aghast at what they saw. Living in squalor and filth, John appeared to be close to death.

It was a Friday morning that the DEA arrived at K&B Drugs and gave Sidney Korn and Alvin Broad until Monday morning to surrender their books. John will never forget the day. "When the DEA finally caught up with them they had like ten thousand blank triplicate prescriptions. The DEA wanted their books on Monday morning. They were up all weekend trying to make up different names — it was an impossibility.

"The government had me nailed completely. Toward the end it really turned snake. I guess if I hadn't been arrested (31 July 1980), I wouldn't be here because I was really on my final legs. I was just a mess."

John was devastated when Bill Cleary was also charged on 12 August 1980. "I was on my way to Idaho when a friend called me from Colorado and told me I'd just made the papers," Bill recalls. "I called a lawyer in New York and he said, 'You have to turn yourself in.'

"'Yeah. I understand that, but I'm not going to do it until everyone else goes through the process. 'Cause you never know.'

"I didn't know any of John's friends. That time I had been in the limo, I met about four people. I never saw a drug transaction. I was always sitting in the living room and they'd go into the back room. I didn't want to go there. I knew what was going on. I knew it was in the bags when they came out of the drugstore. I never carried a bag out, or anything like that. You're a little wary once you're in those situations and try not to make any mistakes.

"I made one mistake when I one time went to pick up John. He asked me to pick up five hundred dollars from a guy. I just knew it was a bad set-up. John told me to come over and pick this up.

You owe him five hundred dollars and he's counting on it.

"'I don't owe John five hundred dollars!'

"'I don't care what you're saying, he told me to pick this up. You owe him five hundred dollars.'

"I wanted to get a little disclaimer in there. So that was it. And there was another set-up that the guy did."

To defend himself, John hired Richard Schaeffer, a former Assistant District Attorney, who had experience in drug cases. "I've been a lawyer since 1969," Schaeffer explains. "When I graduated from law school, I worked as an Assistant District Attorney in the New York County District Attorney's Office. Frank Hogan was the District Attorney. I stayed there for a little over four years. I prosecuted and investigated homicide cases, essentially. Having left the D.A.'s office in 1973, I joined a law firm and I am essentially a trial lawyer and litigator handling mainly commercial cases. But ten to twenty percent of my practice is criminal cases of different kinds — some homicide, some drug-related and white-collar crime.

"It was August of 1980 and I was up on Cape Cod, on vacation. I got a telephone call from Bob Tucker, who I had known for many years as a friend. He told me that John Phillips had been arrested, as I recall, either that day or perhaps the day before. He told me that it was a serious drug matter. Bob asked if I would undertake his representation. I returned the following day to New York and met with John. Another lawyer went to his arraignment when he was first brought before a judge. A friend of mine, John Patton, represented John at the arraignment and made arrangements for him to get out of jail on a $50,000 personal recognizance bond."

Michelle was in Brazil when she found out about John's arrest. "I had got a job in Brazil, and there, on the front page of the *International Herald Tribune*, was the story about John's arrest — the fact that he had been doing business with a drug store and that they had charged him with interstate trafficking. I also knew that Tamerlane had been put into a school where he was living, and there was really no point of me trying to get him back. There were so many hard feelings — there are some rifts in this family that will never be healed.

"During the time that John and Genevieve were very badly addicted John's relationship with his daughter Chynna was completely severed. She spent a couple of years in therapy, trying to understand what was going on and what it meant in the relationship between her and her dad."

John's arrest didn't surprise his first wife. "I thought it was inevitable," Susie comments. "During that period with Genevieve, I didn't see or talk to John at all. It was like a lost love — a lost soul. I didn't know whether he'd come back or come out of it. I knew it was bad. I knew through the family, through Laura (MacKenzie), Jeffrey, and Rosie. We all knew it was terrible. I thank God that he is alive today. I really do because we thought we had lost him — we really did."

MacKenzie remembers the day her father was arrested. "The day Dad was arrested I remember hearing about it from someone on the phone. What had gone on for months before led me up to it. All these things were happening and it was just the realization of how awful everything had become — the calculated risks he had always taken. It finally blew up in his face."

Richard Schaeffer realized, almost immediately, that he was representing a man with serious personal problems. "There were numerous reactions. On one hand, it was clear, when I met with John initially, and the meetings after that with John and Genevieve, John had a very serious drug problem at the time. During the course of what were long four or five hour meetings that I would have with him, he would traditionally arrive four or five hours late. John would be going to the bathroom maybe four or five times each hour. In addition to that he was putting lots of sugar in his coffee — I mean like twenty sugars. It was a clear indication to me that John was heavily addicted to drugs. He was obviously going into the bathroom for the purpose of using drugs. I knew he had a very serious problem. He looked very gaunt. I'd say John is probably about 65" tall. I think when I met him, he probably weighed no more than 160 or 170 pounds. I was concerned whether this man would live to a trial and through a trial.

"At the same period in time I had a number of meetings with the prosecutor in the case, a very bright, honest, decent human being by the name of Mark Pomerantz, who was an Assistant United States District Attorney and who is now in private practice in New York. He was very open and forthcoming about the case and the evidence he had against John — the evidence was overwhelming! I think I told John that short of having every transaction on video tape, it was clear they had a very strong case against him. They had numbers of witnesses — ranging from chauffeurs who drove him in the limousines to New York to engage in the drug transactions, to the pharmacists who were involved in supplying him with the drugs, as well as others who were co-operating, unbeknownst to John, with the United State's Attorney's Office or the DEA. It was clear. The case against John was overwhelming."

Richard Schaeffer recalls John's state of mind at the time and recounts the details of his court appearances. "John was initially arrested and then the Grand Jury was convened. John was indicted on the drug charges that he ultimately pleaded guilty to. After indictment, one is arraigned, then brought before a Federal Judge for the purpose of entering a plea of guilty or not guilty. Certain pre-trial proceedings are conducted for the purpose of arranging or rearranging the bail circumstances.

"We were notified in advance of when the arraignment would take place (4 September 1980) and I told John that he was to come to my office. The arraignment, as I recall, was at two o'clock in the afternoon. I told him to be at my office no later than one o'clock and to wear a sports jacket. John came walking into the office wearing a New York Nicks' warm-up jacket. I had a little anxiety to begin with because John was a little bit late.

"'John! John!', I said, 'you had to wear a sports jacket. We're going before a Federal Judge and I want you to appear to be a responsible person.'

"He just turned to me and said, 'This is a sports jacket. This is a New York Nicks' warm-up jacket — that's a sports jacket.'

"'If that's the way you want to do it John, then that's the way we're going to do it.' We went down to court and the bail condition was continued, and John entered, at that time, a plea of not guilty."

But Richard Schaeffer counseled John that he had no choice but to face the music. "Initially, as I recall, John was charged with either two or three fifteen-year felony counts. It became clear that what would be in John's best interest since he had no defense for the crimes, the only alternative was to enter a plea of guilty. The only question was whether or not John would co-operate fully with the United States

Attorney General's Office in their prosecution of others. John was a little troubled by that — troubled by it only in the sense that quite unrelated to the individuals who were involved in this case and others he had dealt with buying or selling drugs, John had known a lot of people who were friends of his. He didn't want to make a full disclosure with respect to these people who he viewed as innocent bystanders. It posed a real dilemma for John. It was one that we were ultimately able to work through in conversations that both John and I had with Mark Pomerantz.

"John pleaded guilty to one count for which he could have been sentenced for as much as fifteen years in prison. There were no promises or guarantees given at the time he entered that plea as to what sentence he would receive." John was convicted on 24 October 1980 and sentenced to eight years, with 30 days to be served in prison and the balance of the sentence suspended, with five years probation.

The month before he was convicted, John and Genevieve entered the rehab unit at The Fair Oaks Hospital in Summit, New Jersey on 4 September 1980, where John came under the care of Dr Mark Gold, who recounts the story of John's treatment. "Fair Oaks is a private psychiatric hospital that has been at Summit, New Jersey, well over eighty years. Fair Oaks has speciality programs for people who are depressed, people with eating disorders, and programs for people who are drug addicts and alcoholics. The hospital is divided in such a way that each of these programs are very independent and separate. In total, Fair Oaks has approximately twenty percent of its beds devoted to substance abuse research and treatment.

"I was here working on new treatments for narcotic addicted people — in other words, how to get people off of narcotics and how to keep them off. We were experimenting with two treatments, one called Clonidine, which was a medication that was used to treat high blood pressure and had particular promise in helping to get people off of narcotics, and another experimental medication called Nalterone, which makes a person immune to narcotics — in other words, they could use narcotics but not feel them.

"John Phillips came into the hospital in such terrible physical shape that it was questioned, from time-to-time, whether he could walk from the unit to the cafeteria to eat. He had scars all over his body and some active abscesses that had puss coming out. He had liver congestion and a whole host of physical problems that were due to years of neglect.

"One day I saw John in the hole. That was my involvement. I wasn't involved in the admission. He later told me that he had heard an interview about my research either on the *Today Show* or ABC News. John would never consider himself a typical abuse patient, and I really don't think it would be fair to consider him typical for a lot of reasons. One reason would be that he came into treatment in a physical state that would make him very atypical. Not that people who use drugs come in very well preserved. They don't come in looking like they've been to the spa.

"A typical problem for almost anyone like John who has a real addiction is to cure that problem, and then say, 'Well maybe I can try this other drug.' So even though we teach people about this and we try to help them, it happens that a cocaine addict will give up cocaine and will become a marijuana addict. Or a heroin addict will give up heroin and become an alcoholic. Because in their mind they say, 'Maybe I can take this drug.' Our greatest concern is that this will happen, and the person will not only become addicted to the second drug, but will then lower their resistance and become addicted to the first drug as well.

"It's unfortunate but common that once a person has developed a particular substance problem, they focus on it and they say, 'I'm not a drug addict. I'm a cocaine addict, or I am a heroin addict, and that means I can still drink, or I can still smoke marijuana.' Then, they end up in trouble with those drugs as well and sooner or later they get to the 'no' drug position which is what we had all along.

"If someone were to have stopped John and said, 'Look, you're going nowhere but down hill, you're killing yourself, you're a talented person, you can do a lot but you haven't done anything, get moving, get into treatment, he would have been able to do it."

At Fair Oaks with Dr Gold's help, John began to turn his life around, as he explains. "The only way I really did find my way back out again was when I was in rehab at Fair Oaks, with Dr Gold. About half my family (Genevieve, MacKenzie, and Jeffrey) was addicted to drugs at the time. Dr Gold said, 'Do you know why they are all addicted to drugs?' I really don't have the slightest clue except that they had been exposed to them. I figured that was the reason. 'It's like the domino theory. They all want your attention. They like to emulate your behavior and that's why they are actually doing this to themselves. Until you can understand that and straighten your life out, there is not a chance for your family members to do that — to straighten their lives out. A terrible tragedy will occur, inevitably, if you don't go straight.'

"I have five kids — and that was all it took. That one sentence out of his mouth. 'You win!'"

John convinced MacKenzie to try again to break her addiction by undergoing treatment at Fair Oaks, as she recalls. "At the time I was injecting cocaine — shooting cocaine. I was living with my brother Jeff and Dad called. He kept calling me from Fair Oaks and saying, 'Listen, this is great. I'm getting clean, and on and on.'

"'Yeah! Dad, talk to you later.'

"I don't know what was happening, but the phone rang one day and I heard something in his voice that I had never heard before. It was his anguish at finally being clean and looking at the situation a few steps away and realizing that if he didn't step in, then his children would be in the same situation and may not even live. I heard something, I felt something in his voice. I was on the next plane to New Jersey. A week later I was a patient in Fair Oaks.

"We were all living in this big house together. We had drug counselors living with us. By the time I was admitted to Fair Oaks, Dad was already out. He was a counselor at the hospital. I couldn't believe I was looking at the same man. He looked like a distinguished, handsome, Senator with his half glasses on. But he was still Dad."

In November, Jeffrey was admitted for treatment at Fair Oaks as his father began his sentence counseling high school students about drug abuse by telling his sorry tale. John brought to the job of drug counseling his genius for communicating plus his charm. Dr Mark Gold says he was a good one. "John has a great sense of humor. I remember one time that he had Dick Cavett and a couple of other people out here and he was talking about whether he should have his own TV show or a special. He has a wonderful sense of humor and he used it to help other people. I think that the patients forgot that he was John Phillips, the rock star, they just thought about him as being serious in his work and a good drug counselor.

"He was somebody who could say, 'Look, I did this, I fooled myself, don't you make the same mistake.' I thought he was very good."

John used his own experience as a drug addict to get the anti-drug message across to impressionable teenagers. He also brought comfort and help to stressed-out parents, as he explains. "It's funny how drugs turn your priorities upside down, especially heroin. The things that you feel are really important in life and relationship with your fellow man — cleanliness, truthfulness, and all the boy scout virtues — everything else gets turned upside down. The first thing you think about is scoring and you don't care who you have to screw to do it. That's why I became a counselor. I understood, so well, people's stories. When parents would come in, I'd always be the one who'd referee the meetings between the parents and the children. They would say that they went to Florida for a week — 'We came back and the house was empty, stripped. He backed the truck up and took all the furniture and sold it!'

"I knew the motivation for that kind of thing. I had done that emotionally to myself and to my family. I had been the poorest role model as a parent that you could possibly be. I didn't even realize it. The drug is that strong. It takes years to really get over it. So that's how it happened."

John's lawyer, Richard Schaeffer, also saw a great change in John. "I felt very sorry for John. I came to like him a great deal as a human being. He was extremely bright, very articulate, very witty, and very warm, among a lot of other qualities. We had a very close personal relationship that can sometimes interfere with a professional relationship. I think it did in this case.

"I felt sorry for what he had done with his life. Of course, I was a great admirer of the songs that he wrote and he had now gone through a period where he'd been professionally, totally, unproductive. He was a man who, during his career, had made a lot of money. All that money had just gone down the tubes because of all the drugs — he used the money to buy drugs. I did feel very sorry about it and was hopeful that he would be able to put his life back together again, but pity doesn't really explain it.

"Each time I saw John, either in my office or at Fair Oaks, he was getting stronger and stronger. It was clear to me that he had a real resolve both for himself and for other members of his family to set an example for other members of his family to overcome that problem. I had a lot of faith that John was somebody who would be back up on his feet and would not do it again once he had worked his way through the drug problem."

Prior to receiving his sentence, John and MacKenzie made numerous network television appearances on top talk shows such as *Phil Donahue, Dick Cavett,* and *Good Morning America* telling their story. On the last week of February they made the front cover of *People Magazine* under the headline "How They Kicked Their $1-million Habit: One Day At A Time." The response was overwhelmingly positive.

On 7 April 1981, Richard Schaeffer and John went to court for John's sentencing, as Schaeffer recalls. "That morning John and I went down to court together. John was very nervous and there was a good deal of tension in the air. Nobody knew what the judge would do. He had been given a very lengthy pre-trial memo to the court which told a lot about John and a lot about why he shouldn't go to prison and how it really would serve no purpose at all.

"When I appeared before Judge Leonard Sand, John was there with Genevieve, his wife. My recollection is that Laura MacKenzie Phillips was there, as well as a number of doctors, including Dr Mark Gold and Dr Carter Pottash from Fair Oaks hospital. It so happened that it was the very same day that Abby Hoffman was being sentenced, in a State court, when John was being sentenced in a Federal court. Abby Hoffman's case, as I recall, was related to drug possession or drug sale.

"I made a presentation to the court, which basically was a summary of the written presentation, or pre-trial, or pre-sentence memo that I had given the court as to the futility of sending this man to jail, particularly when he was in the process of getting his life back together through Fair Oaks and trying to set an example for his family, as well as for other people who were drug addicted — to let those people know that you can survive these things — you can work your way through them.

"The Assistant United States Attorney Mr Mark Pomerantz also made a presentation in which he told the court that John had co-operated fully. It was actually a presentation that was very, very, supportive of John's position. There was one of the DEA agents present in court that day as well. He was wishing John well.

"John made a presentation to the court in which he essentially said how sorry he was for what he had done for so many years of his life and that he was now trying to clean up his life and trying to set an example for the rest of his family.

"The judge, in imposing sentence, sentenced John to eight years in prison and then suspended sentence other than for thirty days. John, of course, only heard the eight years and not the thirty day part. I think the marks are probably still on my arm from the point that he grabbed me in the courtroom.

"'No! No! John, it's thirty days. It's not eight years!'

"John was obviously very pleased — happy and relieved — as we all were."

Dr Mark Gold talks about the controversy surrounding John's apparently lenient sentencing. "I don't really think that John felt that it was a light sentence. I think that his family was in such disarray that he was concerned about being away from home for any period of time. Remember that he has very talented daughters, sons, and a wife. There were drug problems rampant in the family, and family problems that resulted from having an absentee father. So, I think he was really concerned that any absence from the house, at this particular time, was going to be tragic. I really didn't think that.

"There were a lot of editorials written about this, but still the man was given a sentence, went to jail, and had extended probation contingent on urine tests. Look at his behavior. People talk about relapse in substance abuse — this is a man whose urine showed he didn't relapse. Let's take the two cases that came up in the news at the same time. One was Abby Hoffman and one was John Phillips. How many people would have taken less time up front and how many years of urine testing. One marijuana in John Phillips' urine and he was back in jail for years.

"The fact that John is so intelligent hurt him, as far as his drug problems were concerned. We see the same thing with pharmacists, nurses, and doctors. They know so much that they think they know how to control it and they end up getting sicker and sicker and fooling themselves the most. Frequently, you see people like this having a traffic accident or accidentally killing people — having tremendous life tragedies. Because they are so smart, they figure out each new way to stay alive — to keep the run going. It (intelligence) never really helped him. It was being in treatment that helped. Once you are off drugs, then you can say, 'Well look, I was a successful person before. How can I get it together? Now I have a family, how can I get this family back together?'

"I think the worst point for us was picking up MacKenzie and having her admitted into the hospital, in a wheelchair. I believe that John cried. I don't believe she was even ninety pounds. There was a question as to whether she could walk from just the plane to a car. She was wheeled down the hall.

"The best thing he did while he was here, at Fair Oaks, was reach out to the people of the community. He had a number of high-school assemblies where there would be John Phillips with a thousand, two thousand, kids. Kids that he had to say, 'Look, you know I messed up. I'm going to try, real hard, believe me. I knew Jimi Hendrix. I knew this one, I knew that one — I know the truth, and the truth is that, you are better off not to start.' He brought the house down. When we started to walk in one high school, John asked, 'Are these people going to beat me up with a chain?' It was a tough school. He could stand up in a crowd and they'd be singing, people would be emotionally involved in what he had to say — no notes, just looking at the audience and talking to people. Wonderful with kids.

"I think that John was so concerned about his family. His son and daughter gave up drugs, and were all together with him. He brought the family back together — they were all clean."

Richard Schaeffer recalls going to the probation office with John. "We had to go down to the United States Probation Office to make arrangements for John's surrender, some weeks later, to go to prison. John thanked me then for saving his life. He told me he would be eternally grateful and how pleased he was with the representation, that I had insisted he go to Fair Oaks and get his life straightened out. He would never be able to repay me.

"I thanked him for those nice sentiments and told him the way he could repay me was putting his life back together and becoming productive so we could continue to enjoy his music." And as his rehabilitation progressed, Papa John Phillips dreamed of doing just that, forming another band, The New Mamas and The Papas.

THE MAMAS & THE PAPAS

SAFE IN MY GARDEN

Safe In My Garden

Safe in my garden, an ancient flower blooms
And the scent from its nature, slowly squares my room
And its perfume is such that it is causing me to swoon . . .

Outside with the megaphones,
Tellin' people to stay in their homes
Can't they tell the world is on fire
Somebody take us away
Somebody take us away . . .

(*John Phillips, ASCAP*)

D r Mark Gold recalls the day the New Mamas and The Papas had their beginning. "I remember the day that John brought Denny Doherty and Spanky McFarlane here to Fair Oaks, and they talked for the first time about having the energy to do it all over again — to have the group sing. John really didn't have the energy and couldn't carry a guitar, let alone play one."

What had started out as an idle dream for John became a reality when he invited Denny to join him and MacKenzie in their rehabilitation during Christmas 1981. As MacKenzie recalls, enthusiastically, "We were all living in this house, we called the Big House, in New Jersey. It was like a fraternity or sorority rehab — crazy, all mixed into one. All of a sudden he started talking about putting The Mamas and The Papas back together.

"Then Denny arrived from Canada and moved in. I said, 'You're not going to do this without me. I'll play, I'll sing, you tell me.' I'd been singing with Dad all my life and was interested in a singing career, but I got off on the acting career and went through all that. It was there, it seemed right, and it worked. It was so great to be actually working with my father instead of watching him work."

The plan was for MacKenzie to take on Michelle's role and for Spanky McFarlane, Cass Elliot's old friend and lead singer for Spanky and Our Gang, to become a new Mama. Spanky remembers the invitation she received from John and Denny to join the group. "When John first called, I didn't know him. I had met Denny and had done a recording session with him in the '70s. It was early '81. I was living in Los Angeles. I'd had a country band for six years — Spanky and Our Gang. We played all over California, Texas, and Nevada. I had just quit the band.

"John and Denny spoke to me on a conference call. 'We want to start The Mamas and The Papas and we want you to come.'

"'How do you know you want me to come?

"'We think we do. Get on a plane.'

"It didn't take me long to decide. I got to New Jersey and I sang with MacKenzie and Denny and John for about five minutes. We heard all those over-tones. That's what happened."

The New Mamas and The Papas began touring in March 1982, playing at clubs in New York, including The Other End, before hitting the road for gigs across North America, arriving in Las Vegas to perform at the Sands and Imperial Palace in January 1983. They were also booked to tour Australia that year.

Their tours were well-received by fans, young and old, but for the band, the tour evoked mixed emotions, as Spanky McFarlane explains. "Around 1983 there was a tour to Australia. We'd planned it for six months. It was going to be the entire month of June 1983. We were going to take the continent by storm. Two days before we were scheduled to leave something came up. The government of Australia asked, 'Who is coming?'

"'John Phillips.'

"'You mean, that John Phillips, the convicted felon!'

"We had to cancel the tour and the group really went under that summer. We actually broke up for a year-and-a-half. I didn't think it was ever going to come back together. I went out on another tour, 'The Happy Together Tour,' with The Turtles and Gary Puckett, The Association, and Spanky and Our Gang."

"John hates being on the road — though I thought he loved it," reports Spanky McFarlane. "You can't tell that he hates it because he has such a good time.

"It seems like everywhere we go somebody knows somebody from thirty years ago. Someone always shows up from our past. It's good that they are usually friendly. There haven't been any subpoenas — nothing like that."

During this period, The New Mamas and The Papas entered the studio to record a new album, an event record producer Frank Arraznati recalls. "The first time I met John Phillips was on New Year's Day in Palm Springs. It was a big New Year's bash with a lot of bands. I was walking down the hallway and I heard somebody. It was one of those curved hallways and I heard someone humming. I thought, who's that?'

"He was as tall as I am, so I looked at him eye to eye. 'How you doing?' That was the first time I ever met him.

"He called me about three, four weeks later and said he was looking to do an album and heard about me. He booked the studio and got back in. The man is a genius. He's a great writer and I feel comfortable working around people like that."

With uncharacteristic insecurity, John reluctantly took The New Mamas and The Papas into the recording studio. "More than anything else it was an emotional battle to come back into the studio. I didn't know if I really wanted to record again as The Mamas and The Papas or if anyone else wanted us, being twenty years later. We started recording. I hand-picked the musicians. Out of this vast catalog of songs that I had written, that hadn't been published, we picked the ones we liked best."

Frank Arraznati's enthusiasm for John and this recording session is without reservation. "John was great! He was one of the boys. Actually, the whole band was like one of the boys. Nobody was on a trip — everyone was on the same level. Everybody knew what they had to do, and we all did what we had to do. That's how the project ran so smoothly. It was one of the smoothest sessions I've ever been in on — in my life.

"John's got a wealth of material. We had more than we really needed and had to narrow it down. That was the hardest job, narrowing it down to where we were actually recording thirteen or fourteen tunes out of twenty, thirty, forty or fifty tunes we went through. It was just really hard 'cause they were all really good.

"John is a very good person. I really enjoy being with him and I was really happy to be working with him. In the evening, when we were done in the studio, we'd go over to this bar around the block called O'Donald's. If you know 8th Avenue and 43rd Street, it can be a pretty funky place. We'd just sit down and chat. Of course, John had a million stories about rock'n'roll and his experiences. They are quite funny — don't know if I want to repeat them.

"The album turned out to be an immense project. We really didn't know what was going to happen. The New Mamas and The Papas wanted to do a record and that whole thing can work on people's minds. 'Oh, you'd never be the same as the originals.' We weren't looking for that. What we were doing was trying to create a *new* Mamas and The Papas, some kind of an identity that was there in the past in the '60s, but not copy it — create an identity of its own. If you go and try to make exactly what happened before, happen again, it just never does. If you take what's gone down, pick up the rubble and rebuild it, everything comes out alright if you're lucky. If the material is good and everybody's head is together, then you have another shot.

"John is a very influential writer. He's a great writer and a musical mind. Besides the music being really good, the lyrics were strong and nobody's saying what he's saying — he's saying it from experience. The lyrics are just not heard in pop music today.

"MacKenzie's voice and John's voice have a special thing because it's blood. Scott and Spanky are just great singers. Put it all together and the sum is another Mamas and Papas without Mama Cass, without Michelle, and without Denny.

"John was always the momentum behind everything. He was the writer and he was the main guy. Everybody else just tread around him."

Renowned session player James Burton shares this opinion of John and this recording session. "I went into this session not really knowing who the artist was. It was John Phillips. John was great to work with. He was a great producer. He has great ears, he would give you a lot of freedom and he would like for you to come up with creative ideas. He gave us plenty of time to deal with it."

Although their tours and the new album were critically successful, The New Mamas and The Papas were not so financially and disbanded in August 1983. While MacKenzie tried to return to the cast of *One Day At A Time* — she was fired again after three episodes — Spanky returned to California and Denny to Nova Scotia. That same year John renewed his friendship with Scott McKenzie; they soon collaborated on writing their second Number 1 hit, *Kokomo*, which the Beach Boys would take to the top of the charts, as John recalls. "I wrote a song with Scott McKenzie in 1983 that the Beach Boys recorded in 1988 called *Kokomo*. It went to Number 1 in the U.S.A. and, in Canada, to the hot one hundred chart. It was my first Number 1 song since *Monday, Monday*. I guess every twenty-one years, or something, I'll write one. When I'm seventy-four I'll write another one. But it's coming full circle. It all feels very good.

"Terry Melcher, Doris Day's son, who helped to write *Kokomo* and who produced the record for The Beach Boys, called to congratulate me. 'Wonderful, isn't it?'

"'Yeah! it's great.' I didn't know what to say, really. It made me feel a little better about the whole thing. I guess we were on a roll — coming back. I talked to Bob Tucker (attorney and close friend) about the lost years. 'Bob! The song went Number 1.'

"'After the last fifteen years you certainly deserve it.'"

Also collaborating on the song was Mike Love of the Beach Boys:

Aruba, Jamaica
Ooh, I wanna take ya
Bermuda, Bahama
Come on pretty mama
Key Largo, Montego,

Baby why don't we go
Jamaica . . .

Off the Florida keys
There's a place called Kokomo
That's where you wanna go
To get away from it all . . .

The Beach Boys would also record a cover of *California Dreamin'*, with John appearing in the video as a priest in the church where he and Michelle sought refuge from the winter storm that day in New York when he was inspired to write the song.

With Denny and Scott, John formed an old-style folk trio that toured from time to time. A year later, John was admitted to Conifer Park, a drug and alcohol rehabilitation center near Albany, New York to treat his alcoholism, and when he was discharged, he was anxious to get back on the road with The New Mamas and The Papas.

Spanky McFarlane got another call from John early in 1985 asking her to return to the band. "John wanted to do this again. He called up and I thought, I don't know if I can go through this again — but I did. I came back and I came back for the music. I love the music. It's so much fun to sing those songs. It's really a thrill for me.

"Everywhere we went, every town we went to, John had to get permission to leave the State, and then he'd have to go sign with the police in every State that we were in — give them urine samples. That couldn't be too much fun, but fortunately he doesn't have to do that any more." (John's probation was lifted on May 8, 1986)

Spanky also remembers one of the enthusiastic receptions the band received this third time around. "Talk about highlights. We were working the Fairmont in San Francisco in 1987, and they asked us to sing the national anthem for the opening day of the Giant's baseball season. It was something we all wanted to do. It was very exciting. We started rehearsing and John changed the melody of the national anthem. It was great! We stayed up 'til about two o'clock in the morning. We sang it about ninety thousand times. Then we sang it in the limousine on the way to the ball park and we sang it in the dugout. Finally we get out to the field and we start singing it to fifty thousand people — opening day. They're really excited and we get to this part where we changed the melody and we go into harmony. Everybody started applauding, they really loved it. A highlight? Definitely!"

Music historian and radio host Pete Fornatale recalls his misgivings about attending a show by The New Mamas and Papas in a small dinner theater in Glencove on Long Island. "I was excited about seeing the reformed group, but I was very apprehensive. Was this going to be the real thing or was it just another sorry attempt at capturing some glory past? I went that night with both of these feelings and, as the show progressed, I realized the band still had the goods.

"I think Spanky adds something to the group — absolutely. MacKenzie lives up well to the heights the group aspires to. It just wasn't the oldies which they nailed, it was also with the new material John was doing that night.

"The one thing that I admire about John is his absolute candor about any aspect of his life, good or bad. His life is an open book because of his honesty. I'm glad he's writing new chapters."

Whenever the spirit seems to move them or the occasion is financially right, The New Mamas and The Papas regrouped throughout the 1980s and '90s, sometimes with Denny as a Papa, other times with Scott standing in, singing alongside John and Spanky, recreating the magic of the era, appealing to those who were 'there' when The Mamas and The Papas were the Number 1 band in America and to those who see them as legends of that golden era, as Spanky comments. "I have teenaged children and they love the '60s music. They come to our shows. Other teenagers come and they know all the words. The only thing I can think of is that the parents, people my age, must have shoved the records down their throats or they heard them as baby lullabies because they know every song. It's pretty amazing.

"We have an audience from about six to sixty. Of course, the older people remember. People our age are still coming and they bring their kids. It makes for a big family show — we try to keep it clean.

"John is wonderful to them. If he can escape them, he will, but if he can't, then he's right there for them. They all want to touch him, get his autograph. MacKenzie too — especially MacKenzie because she is such an intricate part of American family life. She's on TV somewhere, every day.

"MacKenzie does her thing and John does his. He kind of lays back and lets her do whatever she is going to do. She's real cute on stage. I think that people are always amazed that she can sing so well. She's become quite a good singer."

In retrospect, John recognizes both the great achievement of The Mamas and The Papas as well as the even greater potential lost because of the rock'n'roll lifestyle he chose to live. "It's been a sort of a wild and woolly life. It wasn't all I expected it to be. I never thought I'd make my living as a musician, even though I wanted to.

"I never thought I'd be a drug addict. I was always very much against it. I always thought I'd be a wonderful, great parent, and it took me a long time to work that out. I always thought that I'd finish college and work for a large corporation somewhere or be in the Navy.

"I never ever thought that it would all work out. Me going to prison, coming out of prison and the road back to work again as a musician, having a number one song again and a new album. All of these wonderful things.

"My family came together and everyone, for the first time, became a real unit after all these years. I had always thought that would come automatically, as part of being here, it just wasn't that easy. There were a lot of curves in the road. I'm just very grateful that everything did work out.

"To anyone that got hurt along the way, or pushed around a little bit, or something — my sincere apologies."

The apologies were accepted and the achievement of The Mamas and Papas was recognized on 12 January 1998 when the band was inducted into the Rock and Roll Hall of Fame and Denny, Michelle, and John took the stage to sing *California Dreamin'*. The era this song epitomizes in music history came to life once again. "I once asked Denny Doherty why The Mamas and The Papas came to an end," Pete Fornatale recalls. "His answer was distinct and to the point. 'Because,' he said, 'the '60s came to an end.' Maybe in a sense that does tell the story of The Mamas and The Papas."

MCA released the
definitive history of
The Mamas and
The Papas on the
two-CD set
"Creeque Alley."
(Album photos by
Guy Webster)

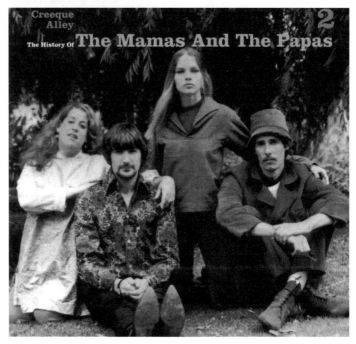

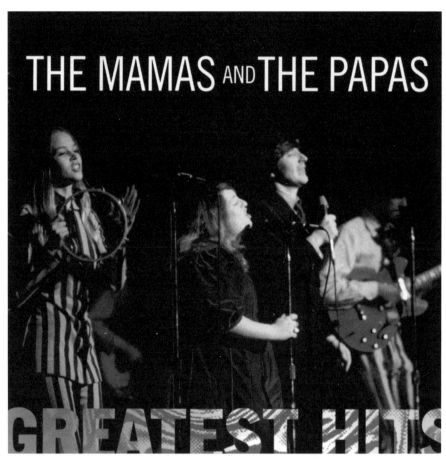

Additional greatest hits CDs were released on the occasion of the band's 20th anniverary and their induction into the Rock and Roll Hall of Fame. (Album photo by Jim Marshall)

THE MAMAS & THE PAPAS

DISCOGRAPHY

THE MAMAS AND THE PAPAS

ALBUMS

IF YOU CAN BELIEVE YOUR EYES AND EARS
(Dunhill LP 5006, January 1966)

THE MAMAS AND THE PAPAS
(Dunhill LP 50010, August 1966)

THE MAMAS AND THE PAPAS DELIVER
(Dunhill LP 50014, February 1967

THE PAPAS AND THE MAMAS PRESENTED
BY THE MAMAS AND THE PAPAS
(Dunhill LP 50031, April 1968)

FAREWELL TO THE FIRST GOLDEN ERA
(Dunhill LP 50025, November 1968)

A GATHERING OF FLOWERS:
THE ANTHOLOGY OF THE MAMAS
AND THE PAPAS
(Dunhill LP DSY 50073, January 1970)

PEOPLE LIKE US
(Dunhill LP 50106, October 1971)

MONTEREY INTERNATIONAL POP FESTIVAL
(Dunhill LP 50100, 1971)

SINGLES

California Dreamin'
John Phillips and Michelle Phillips
(November 1965)

Go Where You Wanna Go
John Phillips
(January 1966)

Monday, Monday
John Phillips
(March 1966)

Got A Feelin'
John Phillips-Denny Doherty
(March 1966)

I Saw Her Again
John Phillips-Denny Doherty
(June 1966)

Look Through My Window
John Phillips
(September 1966)

Words of Love
John Phillips
(November 1966)

Dancing In The Street
Stevenson-Gaye-Hunter
(November 1966)

Dancing Bear
John Phillips
(November 1967)

Dedicated To The One I Love
Pauling-Bass
(February 1967)

Creeque Alley
John Phillips-Michelle Phillips
(April 1967)

Straight Shooter
John Phillips
(August 1967)

Twelve Thirty (Young Girls Are Coming To The
Canyon)
John Phillips
(August 1967)

Glad To Be Unhappy
Rogers-Hart
(October 1967)

Do You Wanna Dance
Bobby Freeman
(1968)

Safe In My Garden
John Phillips
(May 1968)

Midnight Voyage
John Phillips
(June 1968)

For The Love Of Ivy
John Phillips-Denny Doherty
(July 1968)

My Girl
Robinson-White
(October 1968)

Step Out
John Phillips
(January 1972)

JOHN PHILLIPS

ALBUMS

JOHN PHILLIPS: JOHN, THE WOLF KING OF L.A.
(Warlok-Dunhill LP 50077, March 1970)

ROMANCE IS ON THE RISE
(WITH GENEVIEVE WAITE)
(July 1974)

SINGLES

San Francisco (Be Sure To Wear Flowers In
Your Hair)
(Recorded by Scott McKenzie, June 1967)

Mississippi
(March 1970)

Revolution On Vacation
(1974)

Kokomo
(Recorded by the Beach Boys, 1986)

CASS ELLIOT

ALBUMS

DREAM A LITTLE DREAM
(Dunhill 50040, October 1968)

BUBBLEGUM, LEMONADE AND SOMETHING
FOR MAMA
(Dunhill 50055, July 1969)

MAKE YOUR OWN KIND OF MUSIC
(Dunhill 50071, November 1969)

MAMA'S BIG ONES
(Dunhill 50093, October 1970)

DAVE MASON AND CASS ELLIOT
(Blue Thumb Records 8825, March 1971)

CASS ELLIOT
(RCA 4619, January 1972)

THE ROAD IS NO PLACE FOR A LADY
(RCA 4753, October 1972)

DON'T CALL ME MAMA ANYMORE
(RCA 0303, September 1973)

SINGLES

Dream A Little Dream of Me/Midnight
Voyage
(June 1968)

California Earthquake/Talkin' To Your Tooth-
brush
(October 1968)

Move A Little Closer Baby/All For Me
(March 1969)

It's Getting Better/Who's To Blame
(October 1969)

Make Your Own Kind Of Music/Lady Love
(October 1969)

New World Coming/Blow Me A Kiss
(January 1970)

A Song That Never Comes/
I Can Dream Can't I
(July 1970)

The Good Times Are Coming/
Welcome to the World
(October 1970)

Don't Let The Good Life Pass You By/
A Song That Never Comes
(December 1970)

Something To Make You Happy/Next To You
(with Dave Mason, December 1970)

Too Much Truth and Too Much Love/
Walk To The Point
(with Dave Mason, February 1971)

Baby I'm Yours/Cherries Jubilee
(February 1972)

That Song/When It Doesn't Work Out
(April 1972)

(If You're Gonna) Break Another Heart/
Disney Girls
(August 1972)

Does Anybody Love You/
The Road Is No Place For A Lady
(November 1972)

I Think A Lot of You/Listen To The World
(May 1973)

MICHELLE PHILLIPS

ALBUMS

VICTIM OF ROMANCE
(A&M LP 4659, 1977)

DENNY DOHERTY

ALBUMS

WHATCHA GONNA DO
(Dunhill, February 1971)

WAITING FOR A SONG
(1974)

SINGLES

Whatcha Gonna Do
(February 1971)

THE NEW MAMAS
AND THE PAPAS

ALBUMS

HALF-STONED

MANY MAMAS, MANY PAPAS

THE MAMAS AND THE PAPAS LIVE

ACKNOWLEDGEMENTS

This was not an easy book to write but write it I did with the help and support of a number of loving and talented people. Without the support of my sons Mark, who directed, and Gregory, who produced the television documentary and home video, this book could not have been written. I thank them for choosing me to be the writer. It has been a rich, rewarding, and creative exercise. My profound thanks to my daughter Diane for so faithfully transcribing well over six hundred pages of taped interviews. Her uncanny eye for accuracy added greatly to my confidence in what I included in the final text. To my son-in-law, Gordon, who grew up with a love for this music, I thank him for his invaluable assistance and enthusiasm for the book.

Howard Kramer, Assistant Curator of the Rock and Roll Hall of Fame in Cleveland, Ohio, was an enormous help.

I could use a rubber stamp when it comes to singling out Joyce, my wife. Right from the beginning, when I wrote my first book *The Brittle Thread* on the kitchen table, she has always provided her love, encouragement, and remarkable talents for editing copy. Joyce — you've done it again. Thanks.